A Volume in the Series

THE AMHERST SERIES IN LAW, JURISPRUDENCE,
AND SOCIAL THOUGHT
Edited by
Austin Sarat, Lawrence Douglas, and Martha Merrill Umphrey

LAW AND ILLIBERALISM

Edited by
**Austin Sarat
Lawrence Douglas
Martha Merrill Umphrey**

University of Massachusetts Press
Amherst and Boston

Copyright © 2022 by University of Massachusetts Press
All rights reserved
Printed in the United States of America

ISBN 978-1-62534-669-8 (paper); 670-4 (hardcover)

Designed by Jack Harrison
Set in Scala
Printed and bound by Books International, Inc.

Cover design by Frank Gutbrod
Cover photo by Tyler Merbler, *Tear gas outside the United States Capitol,* January 6, 2021. Licensed under CC BY 2.0, https://creativecommons.org/licenses/by/2.0/.

Library of Congress Cataloging-in-Publication Data

Names: Sarat, Austin, editor. | Douglas, Lawrence, editor. | Umphrey, Martha Merrill, editor.
Title: Law and illiberalism / Austin Sarat, Lawrence Douglas, Martha Merrill Umphrey.
Description: Amherst : University of Massachusetts Press, 2022. | Series: The Amherst series in law, jurisprudence, and social thought | Includes bibliographical references and index.
Identifiers: LCCN 2021054533 (print) | LCCN 2021054534 (ebook) | ISBN 9781625346698 (paperback) | ISBN 9781625346704 (hardcover) | ISBN 9781613769478 (ebook) | ISBN 9781613769485 (ebook)
Subjects: LCSH: Authoritarianism. | Populism. | Rule of law. | Neoliberalism. | Truthfulness and falsehood—Political aspects. | Conspiracy theories. | Comparative politics.
Classification: LCC JC480 .L39 2022 (print) | LCC JC480 (ebook) | DDC 320.53—dc23/eng/20220213
LC record available at https://lccn.loc.gov/2021054533
LC ebook record available at https://lccn.loc.gov/2021054534

British Library Cataloguing-in-Publication Data
A catalog record for this book is available from the British Library.

To my son Ben, with hope (A.S.)
For Jacob and Milo, once again! (L.D.)
To Theo and Dash (M.M.U.)

Contents

Acknowledgments ix

An Introduction
  Law & Illiberalism 1
Lawrence Douglas, Austin Sarat, and Martha Merrill Umphrey

Chapter 1
  The Anti-Liberalism of Neoliberalism 16
Sharon R. Krause

Chapter 2
  Uncensorable Speech and the Snare of Illiberalism 43
Elizabeth S. Anker

Chapter 3
  Illiberalism and Administrative Government 62
Jeremy Kessler

Chapter 4
  Post-Truth as a Precursor to Authoritarianism 78
Lee McIntyre

Chapter 5
  The New Conspiracism: Public and Private Harm and
  Immunity from the Law 102
Nancy L. Rosenblum

Contributors 133
Index 135

Acknowledgments

We are grateful to our Amherst College colleagues David Delaney and Adam Sitze for their intellectual companionship and our students in Amherst College's Department of Law, Jurisprudence & Social Thought for their interest in the issues addressed in this book. We also would like to express our appreciation for generous financial support provided by Amherst College.

LAW AND ILLIBERALISM

AN INTRODUCTION
Law & Illiberalism

LAWRENCE DOUGLAS, AUSTIN SARAT, AND
MARTHA MERRILL UMPHREY

Law, Liberalism, and Illiberalism

While the relationship between law and liberalism has been the subject of a rich and detailed literature, the study of law and illiberalism—the subject of this volume—is of relatively recent vintage, born largely of the threats to liberal democracy that the Trump administration posed in the United States. But the United States has not been alone in confronting the dangers of populist authoritarianism. We need but look at Poland, Hungary, Turkey, and Brazil to see that liberal backsliding has turned into a global phenomenon.

Not all of this is surprising. Law, after all, need not be liberal, and legal systems certainly can exist and thrive independent of any connection to liberal principles. Indeed, most legal systems throughout history have served ends unconnected to liberal values; and in the case of some regimes, such as the Third Reich, law has been used as an instrument for the most horrifically illiberal of ends.[1]

But if law can thrive in the absence of liberalism, the obverse does not hold. Liberalism is unimaginable without law. Law—at least a certain conception of it—gives sustenance to the liberal project. In its classic elaboration by thinkers such as Locke, Montesquieu, Adam Smith, Kant, Madison, J. S. Mill, Isaiah Berlin, and John Rawls, liberalism posited a revolutionary understanding of the individual as a possessor of rights that constrain the actions of others in civil society and establish limits on state power. In contrast to the Platonic ideal that identified the individual with the goals of the state,[2] liberalism asks the state to serve its subjects. In liberal thought, autonomy—moral, spiritual, and social—came to be understood as the very condition of personhood. The state was not to impose any particular conception of the good life on its subject, as to do so would be to violate the essential autonomy demanded by the liberal conception of the self. Rather, it was the state's responsibility to create and maintain the conditions that would permit all persons to pursue their own vision of the good life.

As a vehicle to enable the flourishing of autonomous individuals, the state was tasked with performing certain key regulative functions. In Locke's classic understanding, the state emerged as a device to more efficiently and efficaciously enforce the natural limits on personal liberty that existed in the state of nature.[3] Mill viewed the state as the instrument by which the harm principle found enforcement.[4] And in Rawls' influential reformulation, the state served to implement those basic principles of justice that autonomous individuals committed to living in a liberal society would themselves assent to.[5]

The centrality of law to the liberal project cannot be overstated. For Locke, no human space is vacant of law. Liberty, even in the state of nature, is structured and constrained by natural law. And yet the state of nature also suffers from legal deficits, as the absence of a known, promulgated law and a mechanism to adjudicate disputes leaves people in the precarious position of operating as judges in their in own cases; in such situations, Locke avers, men tend to "over-punish," leading to the "inconveniencies" of the state of nature. Once established, the state, with its legislative, judicial, and executive functions, eliminates these deficits and yet remains constrained by law. In a fully articulated constitutional system, the state is constrained by the very law it promulgates, adjudicates, and enforces.[6]

Law that protects human liberty and autonomy by constraining the power of the state must, then, have certain properties. It must be neutral, in that the administration of justice must be impartial; formal, in that the law must cover broad classes of cases; and equal, in that like cases must be treated alike and the scales of justice must not be tipped in anyone's favor.[7] If autonomous individuals are to pursue their vision of the good, they also must be able to plan, and so the law must express itself in prospective norms that allow compliance—an idea that finds expression in the basic liberal principle of legality, *nullum crimen sine lege, nulla poena sine lege*.[8]

Relatedly, liberal legality demonstrates and enforces tolerance, particularly when it comes to freedom of speech. A respect of autonomy and dignity of persons requires tolerating a broad range of speech, for it is through semiotic expression that sentient beings most powerfully express their individuality and sense of self.[9] Law must also vigorously protect speech because it disseminates the information necessary for judging whether a democratic system is adhering to the limits inscribed in its constitution or basic law.[10]

The strength of the relationship between liberalism and law—enshrined in a power-limiting, foundational text; adumbrated by a democratic, electorally accountable body; expressed in formal, general norms; adjudicated by impartial judges, and enforced by a neutral executive—can hardly be overstated. It would be no exaggeration to claim that the liberal vision is unintelligible and unrealizable without the securing power of law.

If we have a clear understanding of what it means to talk about law and liberalism, what does it mean to speak of law and *illiberalism*, the subject of the present volume? While the term "illiberal" is not of recent coinage, its use has grown exponentially in recent years as a description of contemporary political realities. In 1997, Fareed Zakaria published a twenty-page essay in *Foreign Affairs* called "The Rise of Illiberal Democracy."[11] Zakaria described what he saw as a "disturbing phenomenon in international affairs"—the rise of regimes installed by democratic elections yet bent on weakening the rule of law, the separation of powers, and its subjects' civil liberties.

At the time, Zakaria identified this disturbing trend in nations such as Peru, Slovakia, Pakistan, and the Philippines. The past decade, of course, has seen illiberalism take root in Viktor Orban's Hungary, Andrzej Duda's Poland, and Recep Erdogan's Turkey, and spread to Donald Trump's United States and Jair Bolsonaro's Brazil. The illiberalism of these heads of state tends to dominate contemporary discussions of the subject, and the present volume must be read as a response to Trumpism even if only two of the chapters deal with Trumpian illiberalism explicitly.

And yet there is also a long critical tradition—considered in our first two chapters—which insists that classical liberalism is, at its heart, illiberal. Marxist thought prominently claimed to lay bare the underlying illiberalism of liberalism. For the Marxist, the liberal defense of individual autonomy amounted to little more than an ideological rationalization of a system of class domination.[12] Liberal law, then, served—structurally, if not intentionally—to defend and recuperate the interest of the bourgeois propertied class.[13] Liberal law—with its putative neutrality, generality, and formality—allegedly secured and defended the rights of all, when in fact it advanced the material interests of just one class.

Nowhere was the purported illiberalism of liberal law more destructively on display than in contract law, where, in the United States, the Supreme Court historically empowered employers to exploit workers in the name of a formal rights.[14] Crucially, the Marxist critique of liberal law did not claim that bourgeois judges twisted formally neutral law in a partisan manner; rather, the critique insisted that the very formality and neutrality of law operated to obfuscate class relations and to recuperate bourgeois class advantages. A system of formally equal law grafted onto a capitalist substructure based on class inequality simply stabilized and rationalized these inequalities.

The classical Marxist critique has morphed in more recent years into a critique of neoliberalism, the ideology and practice of deregulation, privatization, capital mobility, and global expansion.[15] Whether neoliberalism should be understood as an outgrowth or perversion of liberalism is a matter of some debate,[16] and it is a question explicitly taken up in Sharon Krause's opening chapter in this volume. What is clear is that neoliberal practices invite, in adapted form, many of the same critiques that traditional Marxist directed at liberal ideology. We find, then, neoliberalism accused of concealing and rationalizing illiberal market realities.

The Marxist critique also spurred the articulation of a rich variety of related treatments of liberalism's alleged illiberalism, which our second chapter takes up. In 1989, Catharine MacKinnon published *Toward a Feminist Theory of the State*, a ground-breaking book that replaced class with gender as the key concept around which the critique of liberalism turned.[17] The target of MacKinnon's critique was liberal legality's robust defense of freedom of speech and expression. Just as traditional Marxists insisted that liberal legality's commitment to formal equality rationalized a world of substantive inequality and class domination, MacKinnon argued that liberal legality's defense of tolerance and protection of speech worked to rationalize a world of male domination and female subordination.

Far from a doctrine that encouraged human flourishing and protected the dignitary rights of all persons, liberal free speech worked, MacKinnon argued, to secure and maintain women's subjection in a male world. In the name of tolerance, First Amendment jurisprudence—in particular, the Supreme Court's protection of pornography—legitimized violence against women.[18] In this way, liberal legality demeaned and degraded women, reducing them to the status of second-class citizens. Liberal legality made possible the flourishing of men by entrenching the subordination of women.

Critical race theory (CRT) also offered a fresh inflection of the Marxist critique.[19] If feminist jurisprudence substituted gender for class, critical race studies added race to the mix. From the perspective of the standard Marxist critique, both additions or substitutions were problematic, as Marxist analysis treated racial and gender tensions as epiphenomenal—as secondary, displaced manifestations of the irresolvable structural tensions between classes in a capitalist system. CRT rejected this reductionist formula, insisting that racism answered to a distinct logic that could not be sublated to some deeper structural social tension. To this argument, critical race studies offered a genealogical account, claiming to expose the illiberal origins of liberal social arrangements in colonial domination, ethnic cleansing, forced population transfers, and genocide.[20] Colonial administration and domination, CRT insisted, did not simply serve the needs of expanding capital; its practices were predicated on notions of racial subordination and subjugation *sui generis*.

According to CRT, liberalism's illiberal origins continue to leave their mark on the principles and processes of liberal legality. The liberal championing of individual autonomy and liberty ultimately has supplied a powerful defense of white privilege. Just as some feminists saw First Amendment jurisprudence as a tool that allowed pornographers and misogynists to commit violence against women, CRT sees the liberal defense of free speech as authorizing and protecting racist speech.

And yet CRT's critique goes deeper still. A basic principle of liberal legality is that like cases must be treated alike. This principle is the necessary consequence of a commitment to treating persons as formally equal possessors of an abstract bundle of rights. CRT challenges the very assumption that cases can be considered alike giving the distorting force of racism.[21] In the Supreme Court's oral argument in *Fisher v. University of Texas*, in which the Court ultimately rejected a challenge to the university's race conscious admissions policy, Justice Samuel Alito asked why an applicant from a historically underrepresented class should gain admission over a white applicant if the two were "completely identical with regard to all factors except for their race."[22] From the perspective of the critical race theorist, Alito's question revealed a bizarre and disturbing naiveté. To say that a Black and white applicant can be "completely identical" except for skin color is to utterly misapprehend the very workings of race and racism; the history of racism and its unmastered legacy run so deep in American society that it makes no sense to posit some hypothetical comparison of persons who are identical except for their skin color.

Far from enshrining a basic commitment to fairness, the principle of likeness, then, simply ignores legacies of privilege and histories of racial subjugation. Liberal legality thus reveals its profound illiberality—its perpetuation of practices of racism under the guise of formal equality.

As our second chapter also makes clear, the progressive critique of liberal legality has found support in some unlikely sources. The German legal thinker Carl Schmitt was an ardent anti-liberal, though most decidedly not of a progressive stripe. Once dubbed the "crown jurist of the Third Reich,"[23] Schmitt was an aggressive if subtle defender of authoritarianism. While apologists of Martin Heidegger have insisted that his flirtation with Nazism was incidental to his philosophy and so did not detract from his philosophic achievements, such an argument will not work in Schmitt's case. Schmitt's embrace of Nazism and defense of the *Führerstaat* followed from his legal thinking, just as his jurisprudential writings delivered legal justifications for Nazism. Moreover, his anti-liberalism was inseparable from his deep and abiding antisemitism, as he decried liberal jurisprudence as a creature of Jewish thought.[24]

Long treated as a pariah thanks to his antisemitic and authoritarian writings, Schmitt has enjoyed a remarkable renaissance among progressive thinkers drawn to his writings on sovereign decisionism.[25] As we have noted, liberalism sees law as capable of limiting political power by subsuming it to rule-based governance. Schmitt attacked this liberal vision as incoherent. Political power can never be entirely subdued by rules, Schmitt insisted. Sovereignty asserts and reveals itself in the declaration of emergency, an act of decisionism that, by definition, resists rule-based governance. No legal system, Schmitt argued, can control and police its own suspension. Sovereign power always and necessarily exceeds law.

In the wake of 9/11, anti-liberal thinkers on the left seized on Schmitt's argument to explain and critique the Bush administration's indefinite detention of suspected "foreign unlawful enemy combatants," its use of "enhanced interrogation techniques" on suspected terrorists confined in CIA "black site" prisons, its rendition of other suspects to nations that engaged in widespread torture, and its secret wiretapping of millions of Americans. These practices were seen as powerful confirmation of Schmitt's insight that liberal legality's belief and faith in rule-based governance was so much rubbish.[26] Here again the charge was not that liberal legality was vulnerable to degenerating into a profoundly illiberal system. Rather, the charge went deeper still—that legalism's claim to subject state power to the rule of rules was always and necessarily illusory. Liberal legality necessarily presupposed a basic illiberalism that it constantly sought to conceal and deny.

For Schmitt, liberalism's ultimate failing was that it offered no theory of politics. Schmitt's illiberalism sought to correct this failure. Schmitt insisted that the political is not based on any underlying normative or evaluative system. Ethics turns on the distinction between the good and the bad; aesthetics on the distinction between the beautiful and the ugly; economics on the difference between the efficient and inefficient.[27] The political, by contrast, defines itself in terms of the friend-enemy distinction, a distinction that does not derive its force from these other evaluative systems—the "friend" need not be strictly good, or beautiful, or efficient. The friend is a friend and the enemy an enemy simply by virtue of being defined as such by the sovereign. In this way, Schmitt's concept of the political is tied to his conception of sovereign decisionism. Just as the sovereign "decides on the exception," he is responsible for drawing the distinction that lies at the very heart of the political—he designates our friends and enemies.[28]

This definition of politics, alas, seems peculiarly apt given the rise of illiberal leaders such as Orban in Hungary, Duda in Poland, Erdogan in Turkey, Bolsonaro in Brazil, and Trump in the United States. And yet the claim of some anti-liberals on the left, that these leaders have simply made visible the underlying illiberalism that has always nestled in the heart of allegedly liberal politics, simply will not do.[29] These leaders must be understood as they understand themselves—as champions of a recrudescent populism and tribalism fundamentally at odds with liberalism's dedication to cosmopolitan tolerance and universal rights. Each of these leaders has aggressively pursued a nationalist agenda, one that draws a sharp distinction between the citizen/friend and the alien/immigrant/Muslim/enemy. At the same time, they have brought the friend/enemy distinction to bear in the internal politics of their nations, drawing sharp lines between, for example, the right wing/evangelical/white/friend and the liberal/secular/Black/enemy.

Of most relevance to the last three chapters in this volume, these leaders share a contempt for constitutional processes and have worked to turn the liberal value of free speech on its head, transforming it into a weapon that protects the leader's power to spin conspiracy theories and spread falsehoods. While the liberal view of history is Whiggish, cosmopolitan, and future-oriented—"the arc of history bends toward justice"—the new illiberalism is rooted in narratives of perceived shared grievance, of threats coming from foes abroad and subversives at home.[30] In the name of protecting democracy, the new illiberal leaders attack the separation of powers and the independence of the judiciary. And while the friend/enemy distinction plays a powerful role in immigration policies, it also infects the administration of justice, which is transformed into a tool to protect the friends of the leader and to settle scores with his enemies.

Today's illiberal regimes also highlight how law itself has been deployed to dismantle liberal legality. In Hungary, Orban's government has succeeded in creating a virtual media monopoly—not by ignoring or breaking the law, but by exploiting and manipulating existing tax and licensing laws to permit loyalists to purchase and take command of media outlets.[31] Notably, Orban's attack on the independent judiciary has been accomplished through legal means—by expanding the number of judges on the nation's supreme court, and by lowering the mandatory retirement ages of judges from seventy to sixty-two. This latter change forced nearly 300 judges off the bench, opening the door to the installation of judicial loyalists.[32] And by securing a two-thirds' majority in the parliament, Fidesz (Orban's ruling party) was able to push through constitutional amendments, including one that stripped the Constitutional Court of the authority to review constitutional challenges involving certain parliamentary acts. In this way, the "rule of law is simultaneously followed and breached."[33]

Much the same can be said about the Trump presidency. It is worth noting that one of Trump's most illiberal policies, the so-called Muslim travel ban, ultimately was upheld by the Supreme Court.[34] In pursuing a profoundly illiberal agenda, Trump never acted in defiance of a court order; rather, borrowing from the illiberal toolkit, he installed loyalists in federal judgeships and at the helm of federal bureaucracies. With the appointment of Bill Barr as attorney general, Trump was able, at least until the 2020 election, to turn the Justice Department into a vehicle for protecting friends and attacking enemies, to the point of even seizing the records of Democratic members of the House of Representatives. In his last days in office, Trump aggressively used the president's power to grant pardons to friends and allies who had committed crimes in the service of Trump's political ambitions. Most constitutionalists would agree that these acts disgraced and misused the pardon power but did not violate the constitution itself. Notably, Trump did not engage in a self-pardon, an act that arguably would have constituted a constitutional violation.[35] Trump largely worked within the law to erode the rule of law.

Trump also used the liberal doctrine of free speech as a tool against itself. As we have noted, free speech serves two principal aims—it allows people the autonomy to engage in self-expression largely without fetters; and second, it supplies a citizenry with the necessary knowledge and truths without which a constitutional democracy cannot function. This tradition tolerates uncivil speech, because, *pace* Mill, it holds that truth will expose lies and that the evil of government censorship is greater than the perils posed by untoward speakers. This liberal doctrine, however, was never designed to deal with a situation in which the principal expositor of uncivil speech and political falsehoods is the occupant of the White House, rather than members of some fringe extremist group.[36] But this is precisely what happened under Trump. Trump demonstrated how a demagogue can tactically use a Twitter feed to spread lies about, and so erode faith in, the very institutions designed to keep government honest and elections safe.

But if liberal legality can be turned against itself, can it also serve as a check and restraint against the specter of illiberalism? This is the final question considered in the present volume. While Trump used the protections afforded free speech to spread lies about the press itself, those same robust protections protected journalists and pundits from any would-be effort to crack down on press freedoms. Media sources most critical of the president actually thrived under Trump's years in office, and the availability of information dedicated to laying bare the president's lies and conspiracy theories contributed to two remarkable facts—first, that during the course of his presidency, Trump's approval rating never hit fifty percent; and second, that he was voted out of office by a seven-million popular vote margin. And when Trump sought, in his most dramatic attack on liberal democracy, to deny Joe Biden his victory, he was stymied by the courts and, in part, by judges of his own choosing.[37] And yet even the independent judiciary could not protect Americans from the explosion of illiberalism that we witnessed on January 6, 2021.

The Chapters

As noted earlier, the first chapter in the book, Sharon Krause's "The Anti-Liberalism of Neoliberalism," takes up the post-Marxist critique that understands neoliberalism as the most recent manifestation of liberalism's basic, underlying illiberalism. The very term "neoliberalism" asks us to draw a line from the principles of classic liberalism to the present ideology loosely associated with the championing of deregulation, privatization, capital mobility, and global free trade.

While acknowledging that classic liberals such as Montesquieu and Mill were insufficiently attentive to the threat that economic power posed to individual liberty, Krause pushes back against the proposition that by focusing its attention on the power of political actors and social groups, classical liberalism rationalized and justified the unfettered power of economic elites. For Krause, neoliberalism is less an outgrowth of classical liberalism than a distortion of liberal principles that "object to arbitrary power in any form, whether political, social, or economic."

Krause insists that classical liberalism provides a tool for interrogating the pieties of neoliberalism and that law can serve as a means of restraining neoliberal practices. These legal restraints could take the form of adjudicatory and administrative control of massive and monopolistic companies; they could also take the form of laws that limit the power that corporations and the wealthy have over the electoral process. And yet Krause recognizes that it is not sufficient simply to revive classical liberalism; liberalism itself must change in order to adequately rise to the challenge posed by neoliberal inequalities. She laments that the most effective contemporary movements against neoliberalism are the "distinctly illiberal" ones led by "racist, xenophobic demagogues with authoritarian aspirations." All the same, Krause insists that a revamped and reinvigorated liberalism can work to check the illiberalism of both neoliberalism and its populist-nationalist critics.

The second chapter, "Uncensorable Speech and the Snares of Illiberalism" by Elizabeth Anker, powerfully complements Krause's. Anker begins with a discussion of the anti-liberal critique of Wendy Brown, who, in contrast to Krause, sees neoliberalism as a "clear outgrowth of classical liberalism." But Anker quickly moves away from a preoccupation with neoliberalism, instead training her attention on the discourse-based critiques of liberalism by feminist and CRT scholars and other progressives who have appropriated the work of anti-liberals such as Schmitt. This concern with speech and discourse is taken up again in this volume's final two chapters, which consider the illiberal attack on truth issuing from the demagogic right. Anker's purpose, by contrast, is to argue that progressive attacks on liberal rights and free speech have helped pave the way to the present moment.

In Anker's telling, as "leftist thinkers ... emphasized the violence perpetrated by language, both as an archive of history's abuses but also as the scaffolding of structural and other oppression," the more they came to prioritize speech aimed at "dialecticism, ambiguity, difficulty, parody, and irony." Such a "carnival of undisciplined, unforeseeable, antiauthoritarian speech and expression" would, so it was believed, break free from the confines, binaries, and exclusions upon which free speech was allegedly predicated. This ideology of speech, Anker argues, sought to elevate the speech of the silenced and victimized regardless (or, more accurately, because) of the inarticulacy or contentless nature of that speech. This ultimately proved "self-sabotaging," as it served to evacuate questions of "truth content or normative fiber" from the calculation of speech's value, depriving thinkers of any "evaluative mechanism for assessing when a given speech act should ... be subject to legal ... oversight." Anker bracingly concludes that arguments from the left lent themselves to misappropriation by today's illiberal actors, inadvertently helping to pave the way to our post-truth world.

The third chapter, Jeremy Kessler's "Illiberalism and Administrative Government," picks up where Anker leaves off, with a consideration of the illiberalism of the present moment. But in contrast to the concluding chapters, which examine the illiberal war on truth and its legal consequences, Kessler's focus is on the administrative state. As we noted, Krause holds out the hope that the worst excesses of neoliberalism—the deforming maldistribution of wealth and the outsized power of monopolistic corporations—can be regulated through the courts and administrative agencies.

Kessler is not so sure. For one thing, he notes that courts and administrative agencies often work at cross-purposes, with the former often intervening to check the power of the latter. More to the point, he argues that the administrative state is just as likely to subvert as it is to advance the interests of liberal democracy. Run by officials who, as Kessler notes, may be "subject to the supervision of all the other branches of government, while not being fully identified with any of them," the administrative state is less than democratic; and in its vast discretionary power granted through open-textured delegations, it is also less than liberal.

And yet the alleged illiberalism of the administrative state has itself come under aggressive attack from the illiberal right. Recall Steve Bannon's early pledge to "deconstruct" the administrative state and Trump's endless attacks on a so-called "deep state"—the mythic "complex of bureaucrats, technocrats and plutocrats" determined to undermine and sabotage Trump's populist presidency.[38] The irony, of course, was that Trump deployed the myth of the deep state to purge government agencies of administrative expertise and to install cronies in positions of power. But as Kessler explains, that should not have surprised us. If administrative government is to "work at all," Kessler argues, it cannot resolve the tensions between democracy and liberalism that lie at its core; at best it can reproduce them—without any guarantee that it will be able to so. As Kessler concludes, "presidentialism"—the idea that the executive branch can meaningfully check administrative government through the president's power to select and replace leading administrators—is not a reliable check, if, say, the president is "unreliably democratic and unreliably liberal." The Trump administration made that point all too clear.

The fourth chapter, Lee McIntyre's "Post-Truth as a Precursor to Authoritarianism," takes as its central concern issues touched upon in the two previous chapters. In chapter 2, Anker finds antecedents to the illiberal volitization of speech in the progressive critique of the liberal free speech tradition, while in chapter 3, Kessler indirectly introduces us to one of the most pernicious examples of this volitization—the myth of the "deep state." McIntyre, then, focuses directly on the Trump administration's illiberal attack on truth.

As McIntyre argues, this attack threatens two central features of liberal legality—democratic self-governance and the rule of law. Quoting Timothy Snyder, McIntrye notes that "to abandon facts is to abandon freedom. If nothing is true, then no one can criticize power because there is no basis to do so." The liberal vision of limited self-government becomes unsustainable if citizens take falsehoods for the truth and the truth as fake news. The rule of law likewise erodes if leaders can escape legal accountability by relentlessly lying about both their conduct and the integrity of those tasked with investigating and judging their conduct.

For McIntyre, the Trump presidency delivered a textbook example of the power of illiberal discourse to erode democratic norms and the rule of law. In tirelessly labeling the Robert Mueller probe and his first impeachment trial as partisan and corrupt, Trump was largely successful in evading any reckoning with his transparent abuses of the presidency. And while Trump's baseless and conspiracy-minded attacks on the 2020 presidential vote did not succeed in overturning Biden's victory, they alarmingly managed to convince tens of millions of Americans that our electoral system is rigged and untrustworthy. McIntyre concludes with the hope that "if you can convince a population to be skeptical and think for themselves, perhaps the authoritarian threat can be avoided"—a hope that his chapter asks us not to place great faith in. The danger of Trump's illiberal discourse lies in the fact that it spreads skepticism about the very possibility of ascertaining the truth. As Hannah Arendt put it, "The sense by which we take our bearings in the real world—and the category of truth vs. falsehood is among the mental means to this end—is being destroyed."[39]

The fifth and final chapter, "The New Conspiracism: Public and Private Harm and Immunity from the Law" by Nancy Rosenblum, elaborates on McIntyre's concerns by focusing specifically on the rise of conspiratorial thinking. As Rosenblum notes, "Conspiracism is nothing new in politics." What is new is how it has moved from the "fringes of American life to social media and mainstream media and into the White House." Also novel about the "new conspiracism" is its utter detachment from real events. In the past, Rosenblum notes, conspiracy theories seized on actual happenings in the world, from the assassination of President Kennedy to the September 11 attacks. The new conspiracism, by contrast, "dispenses with the burden of explanation. Often enough there is no event to explain. Pizzagate is conjured out of thin air."

Like Anker and McIntyre, Rosenblum believes that the new conspiracism—insular, dismissive of inconvenient facts, self-validating, endlessly repeated on social media platforms, and endorsed by persons in power—represents a genuine threat to liberal democracy. As Rosenblum notes, such thinking, with its claims of electoral fraud and of deep-state forces operating to unseat the president, works to "delegitimate democracy's foundational institutions."

Can law be used to check or restrain these illiberal forces? Rosenblum is less than sanguine. Liberalism's defense of free speech can be turned on its head to attack any effort at restraint as itself illiberal—witness, for example, Ted Cruz's insistence that Facebook's ban of Alex Jones amounted to a "fascist assault on conservatives," with similar expressions greeting Facebook's two-year suspension of Trump's account. While civil actions, such as suits alleging defamation or the intentional infliction of emotional distress, might deliver a means of responding to certain forms of conspiratorial thinking, in general it is exceptionally difficult to prevail in suits brought against public figures. More to the point, while civil actions can be brought by persons or corporations targeted by conspiracists, they leave public institutions—such as our electoral system—powerless against these toxic attacks.

Social media platforms such as Twitter and Facebook have belatedly recognized the need to curate their content more vigilantly; all the same, Rosenblum worries that platform bans raise classical liberal concerns about who polices the gatekeeper while also having all the efficacy of squeezing a balloon. Such bans lead conspiracists to simply migrate elsewhere. Ultimately, Rosenblum believes that if the new conspiracism is to be "defanged, deterred, and contained," the efforts must come not from regulatory law but from "public resistance assisted by a responsible press and political representatives."

Whether such resistance proves enough remains the great question of our day. Certainly, the willingness of Republican lawmakers to support and operationalize Trump's Big Lie about fraud in the 2020 vote raises grave concerns about relying on our political representatives to safeguard constitutional democracy. Robert Frost once quipped, "A liberal is someone too broadminded to take his own side in a quarrel." As the chapters collected in this book make clear, liberalism now finds itself in the position of very much needing to take its own side. Whether it can do so, while remaining true to its most basic values and processes, is the challenge posed by illiberalism's present threats to our law and democratic traditions.

Notes

1. Ingo Müller, *Hitler's Justice: The Courts of the Third Reich*, trans. Deborah Lucas Schneider (Cambridge, MA: Harvard University Press, 1991).
2. Jerome Neu, "Plato's Analogy of State and Individual: The Republic and the Organic Theory of the State," *Philosophy* 46, no. 177 (July 1971): 238–54, https://doi.org/10.1017/S0031819100018994.
3. John Locke, *Locke: Two Treatises of Government*, ed. Peter Laslett, 3rd ed. (Cambridge: Cambridge University Press, 1988).
4. John Stuart Mill, *J. S. Mill: "On Liberty" and Other Writings*, ed. Stefan Collini (Cambridge: Cambridge University Press, 1989).
5. John Rawls, *Political Liberalism*, expanded ed. (New York: Columbia University Press, 2005).
6. Locke, *Locke*.
7. Lewis D. Sargentich, *Liberal Legality: A Unified Theory of Our Law* (Cambridge: Cambridge University Press, 2018).
8. Paulius Versekys, "Liberal Construction of the Composition of the Criminal Act and the Maxim Nullum Crimen Sine Lege: The Intersection and the Solution," *Social Sciences* 76 (September 7, 2012), https://doi.org/10.5755/j01.ss.76.2.1962.
9. "A Matter of Principle—Ronald Dworkin," https://www.hup.harvard.edu/catalog.php?isbn=9780674554610, accessed February 7, 2021; T. M. Scanlon, *The Difficulty of Tolerance: Essays in Political Philosophy* (Cambridge: Cambridge University Press, 2003), https://doi.org/10.1017/CBO9780511615153; Susan J. Brison, "The Autonomy Defense of Free Speech," *Ethics* 108, no. 2 (1998): 312–39, https://doi.org/10.1086/233807.
10. Geoffrey R. Stone and Lee C. Bollinger, eds., *The Free Speech Century* (New York: Oxford University Press, 2018).
11. Fareed Zakaria, "The Rise of Illiberal Democracy," *Foreign Affairs* 76, no. 6 (1997): 22–43, https://doi.org/10.2307/20048274.
12. Joseph V. Femia, *The Marxist Critique of Liberal Democracy, Marxism and Democracy* (New York: Oxford University Press, 1993).
13. Igor Shoikhedbrod, *Revisiting Marx's Critique of Liberalism: Rethinking Justice, Legality and Rights, Marx, Engels, and Marxisms* (London: Palgrave Macmillan, 2019), https://doi.org/10.1007/978-3-030-30195-8.
14. "U.S. Reports: Lochner v. New York, 198 U.S. 45 (1905)," image, Library of Congress, Washington, D.C., https://www.loc.gov/item/usrep198045/, accessed February 7, 2021.
15. Sean Phelan and Simon Dawes, "Liberalism and Neoliberalism," Oxford Research Encyclopedia of Communication, February 26, 2018, https://doi.org/10.1093/acrefore/9780190228613.013.176.
16. Jonathan Chait, "How 'Neoliberalism' Became the Left's Favorite Insult of Liberals," *Intelligencer*, July 16, 2017, https://nymag.com/intelligencer/2017/07/how-neoliberalism-became-the-lefts-favorite-insult.html.
17. "Toward a Feminist Theory of the State—Catharine A. MacKinnon," https://www.hup.harvard.edu/catalog.php?isbn=9780674896468, accessed February 6, 2021.
18. Catharine MacKinnon, "Not a Moral Issue," *Yale Law & Policy Review* 2, no. 2 (October 2, 2015), https://digitalcommons.law.yale.edu/ylpr/vol2/iss2/8.
19. "Critical Race Theory," The New Press, https://thenewpress.com/books/critical-race-theory, accessed February 6, 2021.
20. Stephen Holmes, *The Anatomy of Antiliberalism*, rev. ed. (Cambridge, MA: Harvard University Press, 1996).
21. Jeffrey J. Pyle, "Race, Equality and the Rule of Law: Critical Race Theory's Attack on the Promises of Liberalism," n.d., 42.
22. https://www.scotusblog.com/2012/10/the-fisher-argument-in-plain-english/.

23. Helmut Lethen, *Die Staatsräte: Elite im Dritten Reich: Gründgens, Furtwängler, Sauerbruch, Schmitt*, 2nd ed. (Berlin: Rowohlt Berlin, 2018).

24. Laetitia Houben, "Carl Schmitt: The Ultimate Illiberal?," review of Benjamin Schupmann, *Carl Schmitt's State and Constitutional Theory. A Critical Analysis*," *European Constitutional Law Review* 15, no. 3 (2019): 599–608, https://doi.org/10.1017/S1574019619000300.

25. Carl Schmitt and Tracy B. Strong, *Political Theology: Four Chapters on the Concept of Sovereignty*, trans. George Schwab, 1st ed. (Chicago: University of Chicago Press, 2006).

26. John Brenkman, *The Cultural Contradictions of Democracy: Political Thought since September 11* (Princeton, NJ: Princeton University Press, 2007).

27. Carl Schmitt, *The Concept of the Political*, trans. George Schwab (Chicago: University of Chicago Press, 2007), 25, 26, 27.

28. Carl Schmitt, *Political Theology: Four Chapters on the Concept of Sovereignty*, trans. George Schwab (Chicago: University of Chicago Press, 2005), 5.

29. Molly Roberts, "Opinion | Joe Biden Is Donald Trump," *Washington Post*, accessed February 8, 2021, https://www.washingtonpost.com/opinions/2019/06/14/welcome-never-biden-era/.

30. Alina Polyakova, Torrey Taussig, Ted Reinert, Kemal Kiri ci, Amanda Sloat, James Kirchick, Melissa Hooper, Norman Eisen, and Andrew Kenealy, "The Anatomy of Illiberal States," *Brookings* (blog), February 26, 2019, https://www.brookings.edu/research/the-anatomy-of-illiberal-states/.

31. Andras Sajo and Juha Tuovinen, "The Rule of Law and Legitimacy in Emerging Illiberal Democracies," December 31, 2019, https://www.researchgate.net/publication/338254402_The_Rule_of_Law_and_Legitimacy_in_Emerging_Illiberal_Democracies.

32. Sajo and Tuovinen, 513.

33. Sajo and Tuovinen, 522.

34. 17–965 Trump v. Hawaii (06/26/2018), https://www.supremecourt.gov/opinions/17pdf/17-965_h315.pdf.

35. "Why a Self-Pardon Is Not Constitutional," Just Security, November 24, 2020, https://www.justsecurity.org/73539/why-a-self-pardon-is-not-constitutional/.

36. Lawrence Douglas, *Will He Go?: Trump and the Looming Election Meltdown in 2020* (New York: Twelve, 2020).

37. "By the Numbers: President Donald Trump's Failed Efforts to Overturn the Election," https://www.usatoday.com/indepth/news/politics/elections/2021/01/06/trumps-failed-efforts-overturn-electionnumbers/4130307001/, accessed February 7, 2021.

38. David Rohde, *In Deep: The FBI, the CIA, and the Truth about America's "Deep State,"* illustrated ed. (New York: W. W. Norton & Company, 2020).

39. Hannah Arendt and Jerome Kohn, *Between Past and Future*, annotated ed. (New York: Penguin Classics, 2006), 257.

CHAPTER 1
The Anti-Liberalism of Neoliberalism

SHARON R. KRAUSE

Whatever affinities neoliberalism may have with classical liberalism—and there certainly are affinities—its effects are profoundly anti-liberal. Above all, the concentrations of arbitrary power it generates fly in the face of liberalism's constitutive commitment to the limitation of power. Yet the anti-liberalism of neoliberalism has been largely overlooked in the extensive and growing literature on the subject. Critics have emphasized the great economic inequalities that neoliberalism creates[1] and its "undoing" of democratic self-government and public life.[2] They have called attention to neoliberalism's corrosive effects on education, agriculture, labor, health care, science, the environment, the criminal justice system, arts and culture, and the media, as well as on the souls of democratic citizens and the bonds of democratic community. The damage to democracy that they identify is real and important but it is not alone; if neoliberalism is undoing the demos, as Wendy Brown aptly says, it is also eviscerating liberalism.

This evisceration is occluded by the fact that neoliberalism has always sought to establish its legitimacy by claiming roots in the liberal tradition and by invoking the liberal language of individual freedom. Because there are indeed linkages between them, it is easy to miss the fundamental subversion of liberalism that neoliberalism is now effecting. Another reason for the neglect is that many critics of neoliberalism are also critics of liberalism and so are not particularly concerned about its undoing. Liberalism certainly does have failings, some of which are explored in this essay, but its subversion should worry all of us who care about protecting people from arbitrary power. Moreover, despite the advance of what Brown calls its "stealth revolution," neoliberalism faces serious challenges today as the harms it generates are increasingly felt by populations around the world. In this context, the weakened state of liberalism has enabled illiberal voices to capture the sensibilities of discontented democratic citizens. The result is that the most potent resistance to neoliberalism is now coming from populisms that often eschew liberal principles such as pluralism and respect for persons while countenancing or even celebrating the arbitrary power of authoritarians. To accept neoliberalism's undoing of liberalism is thus to make ourselves more vulnerable not only to neoliberalism itself but to its most objectionable—and seemingly most effective—contemporary opponents.

In contrast to prevailing critiques, then, this essay examines neoliberalism not primarily through a democratic lens but through a liberal one. I focus especially on the problem that arbitrary power poses for individual freedom, which I take to be the core consideration of classical liberalism as a political theory, a problem that neoliberalism forcefully abets. It is true that while liberalism champions the limitation of power in the name of individual freedom, its classical articulations by figures such as Locke or Montesquieu or J. S. Mill were insufficiently attentive to the limitation of *economic* power. They focused on limiting political power—and, with Mill, also social power—and had little to say about the importance of constraining powerful economic actors. Indeed, some aspects of their work point in the opposite direction, toward policies of noninterference in economic affairs, a fact that has left them open to appropriation by neoliberals. Yet the scale of economic power today and its effects on individual freedom make clear that the logic of classical liberalism calls for principled constraints on this type of power along with that of governments and social groups. It also suggests the need to enrich our understanding of freedom in ways that draw on but take us beyond what the classical liberal tradition offers.

So while the essay develops a liberal critique of neoliberalism, it also invites us to rethink liberalism. I take inspiration from classical liberals to address one of the most pressing political problems of our time: the new forms and unprecedented scale of arbitrary power now permeating societies around the world. Yet I mean to articulate liberalism in a new way for this new time, and the revisions I sketch are not negligible. While grounded in analysis of Locke, Montesquieu, and Mill, the liberalism envisioned here departs from them in important ways, specifically by extending through legal and institutional mechanisms the principle of limited power, and by expanding the meaning of individual freedom. The first part defines neoliberalism and elaborates key features of its rationale, legal infrastructure, and political effects. The next section critically engages Locke, Montesquieu, and Mill to recover classical liberal resources for identifying and constraining arbitrary power, including economic power. The final part sketches elements of a reconstructed liberalism that prioritizes, through law and institutions, the limitation of power in all its forms; adopts a critical perspective on how interests, consent, and rights are understood and practiced; and points the way to a more capacious conception of individual freedom.

Neoliberalism: Meaning, Rationale, Effects

The story of how neoliberalism came about, how its diverse energies and perspectives were consolidated, and how it has emerged as the dominant form of political economy around the world today has been widely explored over the last decade.[3] The diversity within the movement as well as its changing emphases over time, not to mention its tendency to promote policies that contradict its principles, have led some scholars to doubt that the term "neoliberalism" has much value.[4] Yet there are some common themes within the tradition, and once Milton Friedman and the Chicago School came to predominance in the 1970s, neoliberalism's identity as an ideology of free-market fundamentalism was increasingly solidified. At the center of neoliberal policy since that time has been the deregulation of industry and finance; free trade, capital mobility, and the neutralization of trade union power along with the power of individual workers and consumers; the privatization of public functions and reductions in social service provisions; and massive flows of corporate money and influence into the political system, among other things. Neoliberalism also extends market logic and market values to noneconomic spheres of social life such as politics, education, health care, criminal justice, journalism, media, and even religion and the family. This extension works to cultivate neoliberal subjects whose identities, values, and desires appear to legitimate the theory and practices of neoliberal political economy. Because of the self-reinforcing connections it creates between structures and subjects, neoliberalism comes to exercise a tenacious hold on the popular imagination as well as on political institutions and social practices.

At the heart of neoliberalism lies a conceptual ambiguity that has enabled it to upend individual freedom in a classical liberal sense while claiming to promote it. This ambiguity results from the fact that, as Brown puts it, "the liberalism in what has come to be called neo-liberalism refers to liberalism's economic variant" rather than to its political variant:

> In *economic* thought, liberalism contrasts with mercantilism on one side and Keynesianism or socialism on the other; its classical version refers to a maximization of free trade and competition achieved by minimum interference from political institutions. In the history of *political* thought ... liberalism signifies an order in which the state exists to secure the freedom of individuals on a formally egalitarian basis.[5]

Neoliberalism takes its bearings mainly from the economic theories of Smith and Ricardo rather than the political theories of classical liberals such as Locke or Montesquieu or Mill.[6] It is true that neoliberalism has become a political theory—specifically, a theory in which political life is subjugated by and for economic ends—but this evolution should not mislead us into equating it with the liberal political tradition. The political theory of liberalism is compatible with a range of economic practices, including substantial degrees of state involvement, as the Left liberalism of figures such as Hobhouse, Dewey and Rawls demonstrates.[7] By the same token, economic liberalism has shown itself to accommodate not only inegalitarian political institutions but authoritarian ones as well.[8] These differences illustrate the fact that while economic and political liberalism share the language of individual freedom, they understand its meaning and conditions quite differently. In fact, neoliberalism undermines important aspects of freedom as understood in the political theory of liberalism. And it undermines freedom not only as conceived by Left liberals who prize economic equality as a condition of political freedom but also by classical liberals whose understanding of political freedom was largely independent of economic equality. Protection from arbitrary power is the core meaning of freedom in classical liberalism; neoliberalism erodes this protection. The Left-liberal critiques of neoliberalism are therefore distinct from the classical liberal grounds we have for opposing it. Before exploring these grounds further, it is worth noting some key elements of neoliberalism's rationale and effects.

One of the premises of early neoliberalism, articulated most forcefully by Hayek, was that human beings could never have full knowledge of modern economic systems because these systems were too complex and human knowledge too limited. Given "the complexity of the division of labor under modern conditions," Hayek said, "the factors which have to be taken into account become so numerous that it is impossible to gain a synoptic view of them," and coordination by "conscious control" turns out to be a fool's errand.[9] Any effort by government to shape economic policy directly, he thought, was bound to generate unintended consequences and pernicious outcomes.[10] It would also lead to concentrations of power "of a magnitude never before known" and give rise to "a degree of dependence scarcely distinguishable from slavery."[11] Hayek's proposed solution was a "spontaneous" or "self-generating" order of economic activities sustained through the aggregated decisions of individual market actors responding to the price mechanism. This solution would address the epistemic problem while avoiding the danger of concentrated power.[12]

Hayek did acknowledge that such an order would require a complex legal infrastructure:

> The functioning of a competition not only requires adequate organization of certain institutions like money, markets, and channels of information—some of which can never be adequately provided by private enterprise—but it depends, above all, on the existence of an appropriate legal system, a legal system designed both to preserve competition and to make it operate as beneficially as possible.[13]

The creation and enforcement of such a legal system, he continued, provides "a wide and unquestioned field for state activity."[14] This role for the state is what distinguished Hayek's approach, as he saw it, from nineteenth-century laissez-faire economics.[15] Over time, the requisite framework of domestic and international law came to include what one historian describes as "institutions of multitiered governance" designed to ensure the "complete protection of private capital rights" in a global arena.[16] These institutions would depend on states for authorization, enforcement, and funding but they would include legal mechanisms such as "supranational judiciary bodies like the European Court of Justice and the WTO" that could "override national legislation that might disrupt the global rights of capital."[17] In this sense, the elaborate legal infrastructure of neoliberalism simultaneously employs, constrains, and subordinates state power.[18] In view of the complexity of this legal infrastructure and its need for continuing adjustment, neoliberalism has required quite a lot of planning and government action, and it is therefore subject to the dangers of unintended consequences that early neoliberals sought to avoid. Milton Friedman once wondered in passing how it might be possible to "keep the government we create from becoming a Frankenstein that would destroy the very freedom we established it to protect," the greatest threat to which "is the concentration of power."[19] Neoliberalism has indeed fathered a Frankenstein in the concentrated economic power generated by its carefully promulgated infrastructure, and this progeny has now come of age.

There is irony in this outcome because another concern of neoliberalism in its youth was the power of private economic interests. This concern partly drove the argument for insulating markets from direct intervention by government. The thought was that the more state power was focused on controlling the economy, the more economic interests in society would target it for capture. The effect of too much intervention in markets would therefore be a weak state subordinated to the power of private interests. Particularly among German neoliberals such as Alexander Rustow, a prime reason to avoid central planning was the specter of a government that "in its weakness or lack of judgment capitulates to private business."[20] Rustow therefore called in the early 1930s for a state that "instead of being a football of interest groups" would be "'vigorous . . . independent . . . neutral,'" and it was to achieve this independence by refraining from regulation of the economy.[21]

Along similar lines, Hayek worried about "enormous aggregations of power" in the form of private monopolies.[22] The problem with "organized monopoly," he said, is its ability to "control my ways of life."[23] Monopolies should be proscribed because when "we face a monopolist we are at his mercy."[24] In cases where preventing them proved impossible, Hayek recommended "strong state control over private monopolies," although he remained wary of the power this control vested in government.[25] Hayek's ambivalent willingness to regulate concentrated economic power in this form was supplanted eventually by the Chicago School's greater tolerance of private monopoly under the influence of Friedman. Friedman conceded that monopoly power was a problem for a competitive market order.[26] Yet when faced with the prospect of "public regulation" as a check on this power, he concluded that "private monopoly may be the least of the evils."[27] The "fundamental threat to freedom is the power to coerce," he argued, and this threat is found only in government.[28] Consequently, if monopolies should arise as the result of competition, Friedman saw little need to intervene, and from the 1970s onward neoliberals largely looked away from the increasingly large and multiplying concentrations of economic power their policies promoted.[29]

Early neoliberals were right to see the concentration of power as a threat to freedom but their conceptions of both power and freedom were too narrow. Like Friedman, Hayek saw political power as inherently more dangerous than economic power (notwithstanding his concerns about monopolists) because it was backed by the state's capacity for physical coercion. "Who can seriously doubt," he asked, "that the power which a multiple millionaire, who may be my neighbor and perhaps my employer, has over me is very much less than that which the smallest *functionnaire* possess who wields the coercive power of the state?"[30] Economic power "is always limited" because, in contrast to the power of the state, it is "never power over the whole life of a person."[31] Then, too, the ideal of "consumer sovereignty" promulgated by both Hayek and Mises was supposed to be a natural check on the power of large economic agents. In a free-market economy, Mises said, the profit motive that drives business "is the means of making the public supreme."[32]

It establishes "the sovereignty of the consumers in economic matters" because it incentivizes companies to satisfy their potential customers.[33] Under what he called "the democratic system of capitalism . . . the common man is the customer for whom the captains of industry and all their aides are working" so that the "real bosses . . . are the consumers."[34] Mises sought to extend the ideal of consumer sovereignty as widely as possible, arguing that the logic of the market should cover many more areas of life. Over time, this ideal would help to justify the neoliberal toleration of monopolies as well as its policies of deregulation, corporate tax cuts, and other supports for the industries that supposedly served it. Predictably, the conglomerates generated by neoliberalism slipped the grip of their putative masters even as the lingering dream of consumer sovereignty has concealed the spread of their arbitrary power.

Moreover, while the coercive power of the state is indeed distinctive, at least since Foucault the productive power that nonstate actors can wield over individuals through processes of subjectivation, the disciplining of desires, and the formation of docile (and consumerist) bodies has been well established.[35] Even in Mill it is clear that power has an active and potentially tyrannical life beyond the physically coercive functions of government, a point we shall take up in the next section. More generally, one's employer, or the company that dominates one's town, or the industries that supply available food, energy, and transportation may exercise influence over the quality of one's "whole life" in a way that rivals or even exceeds that of government.[36] In addition, the use of physical coercion by economic agents, both directly and indirectly, is a regular feature of neoliberal business practices in certain contexts such as resource extraction, especially where human rights are not well entrenched.[37] In the oil-rich and heavily contested Niger Delta, for instance, Chevron "has acknowledged transporting Nigerian forces to quell uprisings" in its oil fields and "Shell has imported arms for the Nigerian police, paid retainers to Nigerian military personnel, and made boats and helicopters available to them in assaults against protestors."[38] One former Shell scientist referred to these practices as part of "the militarization of commerce" under neoliberalism.[39] Economic power clearly can be coercive in many ways, including physically coercive.

Meanwhile, the notion that consumer sovereignty will effectively constrain corporate actors is belied by experience. This assumption neglects the ways in which neoliberal ideology and the effects of its concentrated power cultivate complacent subjects who acquiesce to their own confinement and exploitation. Harvey describes this development as neoliberalism's "construction of consent."[40] It unfolds in part through a culture of consumerism that generates proliferating desires and teaches us that our freedom lies in choosing among the products that capitalism puts up for sale for the purpose of satisfying these desires. In practice, however, neoliberal policies ostensibly justified by consumer sovereignty have consistently eroded the vitality of individual agency relative to large-scale economic agents and the impersonal forces of the market. The result is that consumer choice operates within what Dale Jamieson and Marcelo Di Paola describe as a complex "sea of agency" comprising interlocking forces and structures that constrain individual agency in ways that consumers do not understand or control and that they cannot, as individuals, escape.[41] This sea of agency affects not merely the purchasing choices of consumers but virtually every aspect of life in modern societies, from work to health to housing to environmental quality. It underwrites the widespread sense of disempowerment that plagues so many contemporary democracies at present, breeding discontent, resentment, and what Brown describes as "surrender to a felt and lived condition of human impotence" in the face of the "seemingly unharnessable powers organizing the world today."[42] Moreover, as neoliberalism extends its logic and values to noneconomic spheres of life and to human identities themselves, it "constrains both choices and ambitions" in ways that stultify human trajectories and erode the diversity of lifeways among us.[43] And to the extent that it penetrates "'common-sense' understandings" so as to make neoliberal political economy appear as "a necessary, even wholly 'natural,' way for the social order to be regulated,"[44] it fosters the conviction that no viable alternatives exist. Neoliberalism's construction of consent is in this respect a form of confinement.

This confinement frequently involves exploitation, too. We associate exploitation most commonly with the labor sector, where it refers to treating employees "unfairly in order to benefit from their work."[45] Yet the word has a wider life, as when we use it in a general way to mean profiting at someone else's expense, or extracting value from another person in a way that brings harm to them. We speak of predatory lending schemes as exploitative in this sense. The predatory promotion of pharmaceuticals also exploits people, and not only those who become dependent on opioids and the like but the countless numbers who are enticed by ads or pressured by their physicians to purchase medications for illnesses that could be cured by basic lifestyle changes, medications that not only come at a high price but invariably generate side effects requiring more pharmaceuticals. Modern food systems are rife with exploitation, as well, in the form of corporate profiteering from "foods" that fail to nourish us or actively sicken us while enriching the coffers of their industrial producers. More generally, the satisfaction of the consumer desires that are aggressively fomented under neoliberalism—for an endless supply of unnecessary disposable commodities, for the cheapest conceivable foodstuffs whatever their nutritional value, for pharmaceutical relief from normal aspects of the human condition or socially generated ailments, for jobs under any contractual conditions or at any cost to the environment and our own well-being—regularly undercuts basic human interests in health, financial security, privacy, psychological well-being, and stable community. Insofar as economic and political power under neoliberalism tend to sacrifice these basic interests for the purpose of enhancing the profits of corporations and the power of the government officials increasingly in their service, neoliberalism is exploitative in the broadest sense.

The concentration of power and the confinement and exploitation it fosters undermine individual freedom and set neoliberalism in deep opposition to the political theory of liberalism. The fact that this confinement and exploitation mostly fail to register as violations of freedom is a mark of how diminished our prevailing conceptions of freedom have become under neoliberalism. Much as the narrow identification of power with the coercive force of the state has blinded neoliberals to the dangers of concentrated economic power, so our tendency to reduce freedom to capital mobility and consumer choice conceals from view the many violations of freedom that currently mark our lives, at least if freedom is understood in the classical liberal sense of protection from arbitrary power. This is not the only sensible way to understand freedom, of course. I have argued elsewhere for a pluralist approach to freedom that acknowledges multiple, irreducible, and sometimes conflicting forms of freedom, including noninterference, nondomination, non-oppression, and collective worldmaking.[46] Protection from arbitrary power is just one type of freedom, but it is the type that classical liberals most emphasized and therefore the type most relevant to the argument of this chapter, that neoliberalism is an anti-liberal doctrine. To understand what classical liberals meant by arbitrary power and how they sought to prevent it, we turn now to Locke, Montesquieu, and Mill.

Limiting Power in the Liberal Tradition

Locke's *Second Treatise of Government* (1689), in many ways the first systematic articulation of the constitutive claims of what has come to be known as classical liberalism, offers an incisive definition of arbitrary power along with mechanisms to guard against it. If "the natural liberty of man is to be free from any superior power on earth," Locke says, "the liberty of man in society" is to be free from *arbitrary* power,[47] which is "despotical" and a form of "tyranny."[48] Locke identifies several criteria to distinguish arbitrary from legitimate power, including consent. Political power can only legitimately arise through the consent of those subject to it, and its continuing exercise must be guided by the regular consent of the people as expressed through their representatives in government.[49] Yet consent does not stand alone; a second criterion of legitimacy in Locke is the "salus populi," or basic interests of the people.[50] The power of government is only "a fiduciary power to act for certain ends," namely the preservation of the "lives, liberties, and estates" of citizens.[51] Power that lacks the consent of the people or that acts contrary to their basic interests counts as arbitrary.

It is important to see that the consent criterion is meant to work in tandem with the interest criterion, meaning that power that contravenes the basic interests of citizens cannot be redeemed by their consent. One cannot rightly consent "to enslave himself to anyone," as Locke puts it, nor to "put himself under the absolute, arbitrary power of another."[52] Locke is at pains to establish the basic obligation of all persons (and powers) to respect the lives as well as the "liberty, health, limb" and "goods" of others. He refers to this obligation as "the law of nature," saying that it "stands as an eternal rule to all men, legislators as well as others," such that "no human sanction can be good or valid against it."[53] Political power "can never be supposed to extend farther than the common good," then, and it should be directed "to no other end but the peace, safety, and public good of the people."[54] So consent is a necessary condition of political legitimacy, both at the origin of government and as a continuing practice, but it is not sufficient. Locke assumes that the two criteria (interests and consent) will generally converge because no "rational creature" could be supposed to willingly "put himself into subjection to another" or invite "injuries" to his basic interests.[55] Yet by insisting on the importance of both criteria in the definition of arbitrary power, Locke implies that choosing one's own subjection in violation of one's basic interests is not, strictly speaking, impossible. Still, it can never be compatible with freedom. This point is significant because it undercuts the neoliberal contention that consumer choice, wherever it leads, redeems the largely unlimited power of corporations. For Locke, political power counts as arbitrary when it either lacks the consent of the people or violates fundamental interests they have, or both. Choosing one's confinement and exploitation cannot legitimate it.

Locke recommends several mechanisms to prevent power from becoming arbitrary. Among these are the natural rights to life, liberty, political resistance, and property.[56] The right to property is especially interesting in this regard, in part because of the general principle it suggests and in part because the way Locke understands it to operate is so different from how it has come to function under neoliberalism. For Locke the natural, or pre-political, right of individuals to hold property provides a crucial check on the power of governments because it is a mechanism for forcing the consent and interests of the people to carry weight. States need money to do anything; without it they are effectually impotent. As Locke puts it, "Governments cannot be supported without great charge," and this need for support makes them dependent on the property of their subjects.[57] The natural right to property that Locke establishes in Book 5 of *The Second Treatise* entails that governments "can never have a power to take to themselves the whole or any part of the subjects' property without [the subjects'] consent."[58] They can, of course, levy taxes; the point is that they have to ask.[59] This is no small caveat. To fund its enterprises the state must continually return to its citizens for authorization via their political representatives. In this way the natural right to property sets a fundamental, even constitutive, constraint on political power. It also establishes individuals, at least in aggregate, as a formidable site of resistance to state power, in effect as a counter-power that pressures the state to be responsive to citizens' wills and to serve their interests.

Under neoliberalism, of course, property rights have been used to amass power rather than check it.[60] True, this power is in the first instance economic power, the power of private firms and financial entities, not governments.[61] Arbitrary economic power appears not to have registered as a pressing concern for Locke any more than it did for Hayek, Mises, and Friedman. Perhaps this reflects the fact that in *The Second Treatise* Locke conceives of citizens as individual human beings, where "every single person" is "subject, equally with other[s]" to the force of the laws.[62] He did not envision individual citizens to include collective entities such as multinational corporations worth billions of dollars whose scale and influence dwarf that of many governments and all actual persons. In our own time, given the juridical instantiation of corporations as persons and thirty years of public policies that facilitate their increasing size while minimizing oversight over their activities, we have good Lockean grounds to worry about the scale and scope of economic power even if Locke himself understated this danger. In a famous passage emphasizing the need to constrain the power of government, Locke points out that it would be irrational to form a government to protect people from one another without taking precautions to protect them from it as well. To do so would be "to think that men are so foolish that they take care to avoid what mischiefs may be done them by pole-cats or foxes but are content, nay think it safety, to be devoured by lions."[63] The same logic applies in connection with the devouring force of firms and other large-scale economic actors today, including markets themselves. If we have reason to constrain political power in the name of individual freedom, then we have reason to constrain economic power as well. Locke's property rights cannot do this work themselves, given how they have been used to create arbitrary power rather than constrain it. One way we need to move beyond classical liberalism is to embed property rights within a legal framework and a political ethos that are alive to the ways that the legitimate functions of rights may be inverted, and that guards against such inversions. We shall have more to say about this in the next section.

Still, there is much to learn from Locke's account of what constitutes arbitrary power. As he saw, robust power is necessary to protect the lives and liberties of persons from invasion by others, but it must itself be constrained through principled and effective limits. Specifically, power must answer to the wills of those it affects and it must serve their fundamental interests. Power that fails to meet these criteria counts as arbitrary; in the extreme it is tantamount to despotism and tyranny. Not all instances of economic power today are arbitrary by this standard, but some surely fit the bill. For example, large multinationals are accountable to the wills and interests of shareholders but not directly to those of their employees, who in most cases have no vote in corporate governance or company policy. Nor must they answer directly to the individuals whose communities may be decimated by the outsourcing of jobs, or whose local environment may be polluted by toxic production processes. Moreover, when the government agencies charged with checking their actions in the name of the citizenry are captured by corporate and industry money, the power of companies becomes increasingly unaccountable and unlimited. Even the consumers who purchase their products—ostensibly an interest-tracking act of consent—often find that their choices are constrained by economic forces that elude their control, as we have seen, and that the desires satisfied by the products they willingly purchase undercut basic interests they have in their own well-being. Locke's account of arbitrary power thus illuminates the anti-liberal characteristics of the concentrations of economic power evident in neoliberal societies today. And if property rights are not themselves adequate to meet this new challenge, the more general principle of competing and contestatory sites of power that property rights in Locke imply, which is nascent but not fully developed in his political theory, is an important resource.

One place to look for the development of this idea is Montesquieu's *The Spirit of the Laws* (1748). He begins from the insight that "any man who has power is led to abuse it; he continues until he finds limits."[64] His solution to the abuse of power, or what Locke called "arbitrary power," is to establish a self-limiting institutional framework: "So that one cannot abuse power, power must check power by the arrangement of things."[65] A separation of powers in government (along lines suggested but not fully developed by Locke) is one aspect of this framework. The liberty of citizens "would be lost," Montesquieu says, "if the same man or the same body of principal men, either of nobles, or of the people, exercised these three powers: that of making the laws, that of executing public resolutions, and that of judging the crimes or the disputes of individuals."[66] Montesquieu's model for the political separation of powers is the constitution of England, which places the legislative, executive, and judicial functions of government in separate hands. In a similar way, the French constitution submits the power of the crown, which is the site of political sovereignty, to constraint by the countervailing powers of the nobility and the clergy. The "prerogatives of the lords" and "the privileges of the ecclesiastics" give them established domains of control in society, and their wealth and status make them effective sites of resistance to the encroaching power of the monarch when he oversteps the bounds of his legitimate authority. Consequently, "just as the sea, which seems to want to cover the whole earth, is checked by the grasses and the smallest bits of gravel on the shore, so monarchs, whose power seems boundless, are checked" by the nobility and clergy.[67]

For Montesquieu, the right institutional framework goes beyond the institutions of government to cover a balance of powers across the political, economic, and social domains. For example, commerce establishes extra-political sources of power that can effectively counter the power of a political sovereign. Montesquieu's support for commerce is motivated in large measure by the potential it carries in this regard. Commerce, he says, "has curtailed the great acts of authority, or at least the success of the great acts of authority" by monarchs because of the powerful sites of counter-influence it establishes.[68] The result, Montesquieu says, is that governments have "begun to be cured of Machiavellianism."[69] Another source of the resistance that limits political power is religion, which can be an effective check even under despotism. Despotism for the most part "requires extreme obedience" such that once the prince's will is known it "should produce its effect as infallibly as does one ball thrown against another."[70] Yet there is "one thing with which one can sometimes counter the prince's will: that is religion."[71] Indeed, "one will forsake one's father, even kill him, if the prince orders it, but one will not drink wine if the prince wants it and orders it. The laws of religion are part of a higher precept."[72] Religion is therefore another potentially valuable constraint on political power. The limitation of power in Montesquieu thus rests on contestation between multiple forms, sites, and sources of power. This plurality includes the diverse governmental powers specified by the political constitution, but it also covers the economic power associated with the landed nobility and with commercial activity, and the social power embodied in the long-established status of the aristocracy and the widely accepted standing of the clergy. The contestation of powers within government and across domains is a regular, continuing feature of all free societies, on Montesquieu's view, although he allows that the particular composition of this contestation will vary.

The limitation of power is further supported by another kind of plurality insofar as the diverse objectives of various institutional bodies are underwritten by distinctive sets of values. For example, the nobility in French monarchy is described by Montesquieu as being animated by the sense of honor. This passion is not anything Montesquieu romanticizes. It is a form of personal ambition that is very far from virtue, but it motivates the nobility to defend its prerogatives against the encroaching power of the crown and to stand up to the king when his demands run counter to the laws of honor.[73] As Montesquieu puts it, "Honor dictates to us that the prince should never prescribe an action that dishonors us because it would make us incapable of serving him."[74] He mentions in this regard the Viscount of Orte, who had been sent by Charles IX to massacre Huguenots at Bayonne but refused to do so, insisting he had found among them "only good citizens, brave soldiers, and not one executioner," and begging the king "to use our arms and our lives for things that can be done."[75] The clergy are driven by a very different set of values than the nobility, on Montesquieu's account, and the commercial classes by still others. This plurality of values adds dynamism to the contestation that constrains political power. While it undercuts the force of the collective will that can be generated on behalf of political objectives, it also helps prevent political power from becoming despotic because, like the intermediary bodies of the nobility and the clergy or the division between legislative, executive, and judicial branches of government, it creates obstacles and motivates resistance to arbitrary power. So the general principle of limited power as developed by Montesquieu points to the importance of diverse forms, sites, and sources of power both within government and across domains, and it calls for a plurality of values for the purpose of supporting regular contestation among powers.

This account gives us additional grounds to worry about the regime of neoliberalism. While commerce for Montesquieu was one among several sites of countervailing power useful for checking the power of the government, it has become a power that itself badly needs to be checked, not only because of the threat it poses in itself but also in view of the influence it increasingly wields over political power. The effect of this capture is to gut the ideal of competing powers by infusing them all with the growing power of private firms and industries. This development melds economic and political power into a single conglomeration that presents itself as rooted in the people but answers above all to the wills and interests of large-scale economic actors. We also have reason to worry about the collapse of separate powers across domains, as corporate influence permeates more and more parts of our societies. When universities, media outlets, voluntary associations, and even churches run on money from the Koch brothers and other corporate interests, their efficacy as countervailing sites of power is compromised. Finally, insofar as market rationality becomes pervasive across domains and identities, it tends to undercut the pluralism of values that Montesquieu found so important to the limitation of power. Indeed, the more our values are colonized by the purposes of *homo economicus*, above all consumerism, the more vulnerable we become to confinement and exploitation by corporate power. The narrowing of our values undercuts the limitation of power and threatens individual freedom.

If Locke and Montesquieu were focused on the limitation of political power, J. S. Mill gives us an explicitly liberal argument for extending this principle beyond government. It is true that he does not apply the principle to the limitation of economic power per se. In fact, in his work on political economy he recommends against state-based regulation of markets and economic interests.[76] Then, too, the notion of the "marketplace of ideas" commonly attributed to him, albeit wrongly, seems to import economic rationality into the social and political domains.[77] Yet the core idea of his political theory, articulated in *On Liberty* (1859), is the insight that however important the limitation of political power may be, it is not nearly enough to sustain individual freedom. The dangers of arbitrary power—in particular, majority tyranny—are not restricted to what "political functionaries" may do.[78] Social power too needs to be constrained. Indeed, "society can and does execute its own mandates; and if it issues wrong mandates instead of right, or any mandates at all in things with which it ought not to meddle, it practices a social tyranny more formidable than many kinds of political oppression."[79] In contrast to the political power of governments, Mill says, social power penetrates "more deeply into the details of life," influencing our feelings, desires, and beliefs, and "enslaving the soul itself."[80] Protections against the power of government therefore must be supplemented with protections "against the tyranny of prevailing opinion and feeling, against the tendency of society to impose, by other means than civil penalties, its own ideas and practices as rules of conduct on those who dissent from them . . . and compel all characters to fashion themselves upon the model of its own."[81] Mill's concern about arbitrary social power is one we should share; he was right about the depth of its effects, and his analysis is a forceful corrective to the overly narrow conception of power in Hayek and Friedman. Today the force of social media and other communications technologies has vastly strengthened the power of society relative to individuals, and their often corrosive influence on our thinking, actions, and identities is increasingly evident. This power, like the power of governments, is more and more shaped by the economic power of private firms, a dynamic exemplified by Facebook, Instagram, and Google, among others. And however seductive it may be, social power today is often arbitrary in its exploitative construction of consent and its disregard for fundamental human interests from privacy to truth.

So the political theory of classical liberalism gives us multiple grounds to resist the concentrated and often arbitrary forms of economic power that neoliberalism generates. Indeed, classical liberalism gives us reasons to object to arbitrary power in any form, whether political, social, or economic. Insofar as neoliberalism produces and defends arbitrary power, then, it is a deeply anti-liberal doctrine. Moreover, its infusion of economic values and rationality into noneconomic domains of life undercuts the liberal commitment to a plurality of values and helps facilitate the confinement and exploitation of individuals. In all these ways, neoliberalism turns its back on individual freedom, the *sine qua non* of classical liberalism. If Locke, Montesquieu, and Mill help us see the anti-liberal character of neoliberalism, however, we will need to go beyond them to counter it. Undoing neoliberalism for the purpose of protecting individual freedom requires revisions to liberalism itself.

Toward a New (But Not Neo) Liberalism

Above all, protecting individual freedom today calls for substantially more in the way of legal and institutional checks on economic power. This means setting principled limitations on the scale of private firms, including preventing large-scale mergers and monopolies. This will require the use of state power in all its forms, from the regulatory power of the executive branch to the lawmaking power of legislatures and the adjudicatory power of the courts. Law has been a key instrument in the formation of neoliberalism, as we saw in this chapter's first section, and law is needed to undo it. In addition to the scale of economic power, its scope also needs to be contained, meaning legal limitations on the kinds of things that companies are permitted to do. This includes, for example, restricting their ability to harm the environment and the people whose well-being depends on clean water, soil, and air. It means preventing the exploitation of workers by setting a reasonable minimum wage and more robust health and safety guidelines for dangerous industries. It also means establishing more transparency about the production and impact of the foods we are sold; it means de-incentivizing the practice of planned obsolescence that traps us in an endless cycle of buying and dumping things; and it means preventing predatory lending and the predatory promotion of pharmaceuticals. It will also require new privacy rights and limits on social media. The goal is to prevent economic power from being arbitrary in Locke's sense by forcing it to track not only the choices but also the basic interests of the people it affects. In order for state power to operate as an effective check on economic power, however, we must also get corporate money out of politics, as so many others have argued, by limiting the size of campaign donations and restricting them to individual citizens, by constraining indirect contributions to campaigns and efforts to influence political outcomes, and by ending dark money and corporate lobbying. In other words, we must establish in law the independence of political and economic power so that they can check and balance one another, as Montesquieu envisioned, in a climate of healthy contestation.[82]

The state is not the only resource we have for constraining corporate power, of course, and it must be combined with other forms of countervailing influence. Trade unions are crucial here, although for them to regain the strength they need to be effective checks on companies, a generation of anti-union court decisions, legislative initiatives, and executive orders need to be reversed. In a similar way, companies must be legally prohibited from requiring arbitration and noncompete agreements as conditions of employment. These practices undercut the ability of workers to act individually and in groups as checks on the power of corporations; limiting economic power means establishing in law the conditions that enable workers to constrain it. The mechanism of class-action lawsuits also can empower groups of average citizens, such as neighbors in a community whose water has been polluted by a local mine or agricultural enterprise, to operate as a check on corporate action; legal initiatives that constrain the possibility of class-action lawsuits therefore also must be reversed.[83]

More generally, efforts to pluralize the economy through the development of noncapitalist types of production and exchange could help limit the power of corporations by multiplying both the sites and the forms of economic activity available to us, hence multiplying sources of countervailing power. Such alternatives could exist alongside some capitalist practices in what J. K. Gibson-Graham refers to as a more "diverse" economy. Many examples already exist, if only in nascent form. They include

> the exchange of commodities between and within worker cooperatives, where prices are set to enhance the sustainability of the cooperative; the ethical or "fair" trade of products, where producers and consumers agree on price levels that will sustain certain livelihood practices; [and] local trading systems and alternative currencies that foster local interdependency and sustainability.[84]

Contemporary food movements, farmers' markets, transition towns, and decentralized energy grids offer additional examples of alternative economic relationships that reduce the role of large corporations in the production and exchange of important goods while empowering individuals and noncorporate groups.[85] In the near term, small producers and alternative sites of exchange will need the support of law and public policy to compete successfully with today's corporate behemoths, and all such efforts will need to be matched with stronger legal restrictions on mergers and monopolies.[86] Yet large corporations themselves regularly benefit from state support in both direct and indirect ways, from tax breaks to bailouts to publicly funded R&D to policies that protect them from paying for the costs of cleaning up their environmental messes or treating the human illnesses caused by their products. Redirecting some of this support to foster a more diverse economy is one way to set principled constraints on the scale and capacities of economic power and thereby to sustain a more robust balance of power across domains.[87]

Along with legal, structural, and regulatory changes, we need to cultivate a more nuanced sensibility about the criteria that define arbitrary power—namely, interests and consent—and about the diverse ways that power can operate. This sensibility needs to become second nature to us as a society and as individuals. As we have seen, part of the force of neoliberalism comes from its ability to present itself as answering to the interests and consent of consumers. Yet if satisfying the desires fostered by neoliberalism undermines fundamental human interests, this satisfaction of desire should not prevent the power that underwrites it from counting as arbitrary. We need to bring a more critical lens to bear in assessing our own interests and the degree to which they are being served. Likewise, insofar as neoliberalism constructs consent in ways that generate individual exploitation and facilitate the capture of democratic governments, the "consent" it claims should ring hollow with us. One of the deficiencies of liberalism in the past has been its tendency to overlook the fact that consent and the appeal to interests can mask arbitrary power, thereby perpetuating it, whether in the domain of employment contracts or gender relations or racial inequality. This myopia has made liberalism guilty of what Brown describes as "legitimating, cloaking, and mystifying" violations of freedom in multiple registers.[88] We can resist neoliberalism and improve liberalism by bringing a more critical perspective to bear on both interests and consent, evaluating with a more discerning eye the background of power relations that shape them and profit from them. We must also be more attuned to the subtle operations of nongovernmental power, most of which looks and feels different from the overtly coercive force of states. This kind of critical sensibility is challenging, especially for people who are in many ways privileged and prosperous, because it requires facing the painful fact of our own subjugation. It also demands good faith, skilled judgment, and continuing contestation. Yet the effective limitation of power depends on such a critical sensibility, which means that nourishing this sensibility is crucial to individual freedom.

We will need to cultivate an equally critical practice of rights. Rights are an important resource that law offers for checking power, whether in the form of civil and political rights, such as the rights to vote and to free speech and assembly, or social and economic rights, such as the rights to a living wage, to a decent education, and to organize for collective bargaining. Rights are important both because of the legal limitations they establish on political, economic, and social power, and also because they can support robust contestation by citizens who use their rights to mobilize for collective action on issues that matter to them. Yet just as we must be alive to the ways that our interests and consent can be coopted, we need to be more attuned to how rights may be mobilized to enhance large-scale powers rather than check them. Jessica Whyte's account of how neoliberalism has used rights to enshrine protections for global capital while seeming to protect people illuminates this danger. Whyte details how Hayek, Friedman, and others involved in the remaking of Chile's economy under Pinochet used the language of human rights to enshrine "the rights of private enterprise," insulating markets, corporations, and the wealthy from political pressure by citizens who supported things like public education and welfare provisions.[89] In this context, even "what first appear to be social and economic rights (to health, education, and social security) are actually rights of private enterprise to compete in offering relevant services on the same terms as the state." Thus "the right to education" has given "private companies free rein in establishing education providers," the result of which "has been the 'prevalence of private education' in Chile."[90]

The use of rights as a mechanism for entrenching neoliberalism in law has been widespread. Think of Margaret Thatcher justifying the privatization of public housing in the 1980s "as a way to secure human rights,"[91] or the US Supreme Court's use of the right to free speech, in its *Citizens United* decision, to legally buttress the force of corporations and overwhelm the voices of actual citizens in political decision-making. In a more recent decision, very much in keeping with the dynamic Whyte describes, the Court ruled that union organizing among California farmworkers at the worksite "grants labor organizations a right to invade growers' property," thereby violating the Constitution's Fifth Amendment, specifically the "takings clause," which holds that private property may not be "taken for public use, without just compensation."[92] Important as they are as resources for the limitation of power, then, rights can also be used to legally entrench consolidations of power. We need to be vigilant about ensuring that our legal instantiation and practices of rights actually support rather than erode the limitation of power, and we must be flexible about adjusting the laws when we find that this is not the case.

Critical practices of consent, interest, and rights point the way to a more capacious conception of individual freedom. They focus us on resistance to arbitrary power, much as classical liberals did; but in contrast to classical liberalism, they deepen our understanding of the often "stealth" ways that arbitrary power operates. They make us aware of our own acquiescence to such power and attune us to the confinement and exploitation that accompany the satisfaction of many of our desires. And they illuminate what Rom Coles has called the "Wizard of Oz effect" that makes us feel powerless in the face of a neoliberal order that presents itself, however falsely, as inevitable and intractable.[93] In all these ways, the liberalism envisioned here is compatible with the democratic politics that Brown champions in her critique of neoliberalism.[94] Among other things, it would involve "enhancing the capacity of citizens to share power and hence, collaboratively govern themselves."[95]

In contrast to Brown's vision, however, this new (but not neo) liberalism highlights the limitation and not only the democratization of power. The democratization of power is a good thing, but it is not the only important thing for individual freedom. To be sure, liberalism without democracy cannot reliably fulfill its promise to respect the freedom and equality of *all*; it is bound to be riven by injustice. Then, too, the legal and institutional mechanisms intended to limit power are never self-actuating but always depend on the actions of individuals and collectively mobilized groups. In this sense, liberalism needs a democratically engaged citizenry not simply as a supplement but constitutively, to fulfill its own functions and aspirations. Yet democracy without liberalism lacks a constitutive attachment to the limitation of power, including the power of the people themselves, who have too often succumbed to the temptations of majority tyranny and let democracy run afoul of individual freedom.[96]

Freedom is not the only objective we should have in politics; goals such as justice, peace, and human flourishing also matter. And the particular form of freedom explored here, which centers on protecting individuals from arbitrary power, is not the only form of freedom we should value. A pluralist appreciation of freedom's multiplicity attunes us to the diverse, irreducible, sometimes conflicting experiences that comprise it. These experiences will include collective worldmaking, conceived as collaborative self-determination or action in concert for public ends. They will also encompass individual and group-based struggle against the subjectivating power that surreptitiously shapes us into tools of corporate profiteering and apologists for neoliberal abuses. Yet the freedom of persons to live fully as the distinctive individuals they are, within bounds set by the mutual freedom of all, protected from arbitrary power—this freedom is irreplaceable in the scheme of things that matter, or should matter, to all of us.

Moreover, whatever the deficits of liberalism, one of its strengths is the attention it gives to law and institutions, especially legal and institutional checks on power. We very much need such checks. There is no doubt that the limitation of power also requires radical instantiations of democratic action in the form of mobilized citizens who contest particular concentrations of power in "fugitive" or extra-institutional ways, as in the Occupy movement, or the Arab Spring, or Black Lives Matter.[97] Still, fugitive democracy cannot sustain freedom on its own—not only because law and institutions are needed in order to carry out the mundane business of ordering a free society but also because freedom depends as much on what people cannot do to one another as it does on what we are all able to do together. Ensuring that there are some things people cannot do means establishing limits on power in our laws and institutions. The more capacious freedom envisioned here combines practices for legally and institutionally constraining power in all its forms with a critical ethos that continually interrogates these practices. This ethos also attunes us to the dangers of confinement and exploitation, and it refuses to accept that they can be redeemed by the satisfaction of consumer desires.

Undoing neoliberalism may seem like an impossible dream, and critics of neoliberalism regularly succumb to "civilizational despair" in the face of the "paralyzing conundrums" and "seemingly unharnessable powers" created by a generation of neoliberal policies.[98] Yet to accept this impression of neoliberalism as an implacable order is to fall prey to its own promotional branding. One of the common themes in accounts of the history of neoliberalism is that neoliberalism is the product of distinct decisions made by individuals and collectivities over time, written into laws and public policies. The laws and policies that gave birth to it and continue to sustain it can be changed. Moreover, as invincible as neoliberalism may seem, there are clear fracture lines in its façade today. The resentments articulated by populations in many parts of the world about the effects of neoliberal policies evince these cracks—whether it is the white working class of advanced democracies who have lost jobs to outsourcing, or laborers protesting dirty, unsafe working conditions in the developing world, or millennials with college degrees who cannot make ends meet even while working multiple jobs, or Indigenous communities organizing to protect their native lands from corporate extractivism. Neoliberalism is precarious at present. Precarity is not collapse, of course; neoliberalism is a long way from that. But its current vulnerability offers an opportunity for intervention and reconstruction.

Unfortunately, the most effective movements against neoliberalism on the contemporary scene are populist ones led by racist, xenophobic demagogues with authoritarian aspirations. These forces are distinctly illiberal even as they mobilize citizens in the name of taking back their democracies and reasserting collective control. And in the United States, the populism of Trump coincided with the escalating erosion of limits on economic power and on executive political power as well. Neoliberalism can be reversed, but to achieve this change in a freedom-enhancing way we need liberal and not only democratic mobilizations. We need to recognize the monstrous progeny that neoliberalism has fathered (to return to Friedman's Frankenstein metaphor), meaning the fundamental threat it poses to our freedom, and we need to remember the link between freedom and the limitation of power. We should not take liberalism as we found it, because liberalism itself needs to be reconceived in important ways if it is to make good on the emancipatory potential it carries, and we should be pluralists about freedom in the sense of appreciating its variety, but we should take up the resources that liberalism offers for identifying and constraining arbitrary power. The challenges here are immense, but they are not insurmountable because there is nothing inevitable about neoliberalism, or about any legal and political order. As liberals from Locke to Montesquieu to Mill remind us, law and politics are not established by God or given by nature. They are the products of people's continuing reflection and choice, which means that—for worse and for better—they can always be "undone."

Notes

1. David Harvey, *A Brief History of Neoliberalism* (Oxford: Oxford University Press, 2007); Thomas Piketty, *Capital in the Twenty-First Century* (Cambridge, MA: Harvard University Press), 2017.

2. Wendy Brown, *Undoing the Demos: Neoliberalism's Stealth Revolution* (Brooklyn: Zone, 2015). See also, among others, Bonnie Honig, *Public Things: Democracy in Disrepair* (New York: Fordham University Press, 2017); Jodi Dean, *Democracy and Other Neoliberal Fantasies: Communicative Capitalism and Left Politics* (Durham, NC: Duke University Press, 2009); and Romand Coles, *Visionary Pragmatism: Radical and Ecological Democracy in Neoliberal Times* (Durham, NC: Duke University Press, 2016).

3. See, for example, Daniel Stedman Jones, *Masters of the Universe: Hayek, Friedman and the Birth of Neoliberal Politics* (Princeton, NJ: Princeton University Press, 2012); Quinn Slobodian, *Globalists: The End of Empire and the Birth of Neoliberalism* (Cambridge, MA: Harvard University Press, 2018); Philip Mirowski and Dieter Plehwe, eds., *The Road from Mont Pèlerin: The Making of the Neoliberal Thought Collective* (Cambridge, MA: Harvard University Press, 2009); Manfred B. Steger and Ravi K. Roy, *Neoliberalism: A Brief History* (Oxford: Oxford University Press, 2010); Niklas Olsen, *The Sovereign Consumer: A New Intellectual History of Neoliberalism* (Cham, Switzerland: Palgrave Macmillan, 2018); Angus Burgin, *The Great Persuasion: Reinventing Free Markets since the Depression* (Cambridge, MA: Harvard University Press, 2012); Nicholas Wapshott, *Keynes Hayek: The Clash That Defined Modern Economics* (New York: Norton, 2011); Sean Phelan and Simon Dawes, "Liberalism and Neoliberalism," *Oxford Research Encyclopedia of Communication* (February 2018): DOI: 10.1093/acrefore/9780190228613.013.176; Edward N. Megay, "Anti-Pluralist Liberalism: The German Neoliberals," *Political Science Quarterly* 85, no. 3 (September 1970): 422–42; Jennifer Burns, "Across the Great Divide: Free Markets from Left to Right," *Modern Intellectual History* 11, no. 1 (2014): 253–65; and Harvey, *A Brief History of Neoliberalism*.

4. As Harvey puts it, there are "enough contradictions" in connection with neoliberal responses to monopoly power and market failures "to render evolving neoliberal practices . . . unrecognizable in relation to . . . neoliberal doctrine" (Harvey, *A Brief History of Neoliberalism*, 21, and see 19, 67–70). Burns insists that the "nomenclature of neoliberalism" is "an overtheorized term that lacks a historically specific constituency and has been applied haphazardly to nearly every feature of the globalized modern world" (Burns, "Across the Great Divide," 260); and Phelan and Dawes remark on the "contested and

nebulous quality" of the category (Phelan and Dawes, "Liberalism and Neoliberalism," 3). Stedman Jones likewise finds that the term "neoliberalism" has been used with "lazy imprecision" in "both popular debate and academic scholarship" (Stedman Jones, *Masters of the Universe*, 10; and see Rachel Turner, *Neo-Liberal Ideology: History, Concepts and Policies* [Edinburgh: Edinburgh University Press, 2008], cited in Stedman Jones, 347).

5. Wendy Brown, "Neoliberalism and the End of Liberal Democracy," *theory & event* 7, no. 1 (2003): doi:10.1353/tae.2003.0020: 2.

6. Friedman, for example, identifies liberalism as a late eighteenth- and early nineteenth-century view that emphasized "laissez faire at home" and "free trade abroad" as the means for "reducing the role of the state in economic affairs" (Milton Friedman, *Capitalism and Freedom* [Chicago: University of Chicago Press, 2002], 5). He does acknowledge that "in political matters" liberalism "supported the development of representative government and parliamentary institutions, reduction in the arbitrary power of the state, and protection of the civil freedoms of individuals" (5). Still, his interest in political institutions is limited to how they can best facilitate a free-market economic system. Hayek too defines "liberalism" in terms of "the principles of economic policy of the nineteenth century" that emphasized "above all the principle of laissez faire" and "the impersonal and anonymous mechanism of the market" (F. A. Hayek, *The Road to Serfdom* [Chicago: University of Chicago Press, 2007], 71, 73). He himself rejects a strictly laissez-faire approach, but he identifies his inspiration as the nineteenth-century economic theories associated with that ideal.

7. See, for example, L. T. Hobhouse, *Liberalism and Other Writings* (Cambridge: Cambridge University Press, 1994), esp. chaps. 4 and 8; John Dewey, *Liberalism and Social Action* (Amherst, MA: Prometheus Books, 1991) and *Individualism Old and New* (Amherst, MA: Prometheus Books, 1984), esp. chaps. 2 and 6; John Rawls, *Justice as Fairness: A Restatement* (Cambridge, MA: Harvard University Press, 2001), esp. part II; and Phelan and Dawes, "Liberalism and Neoliberalism," 5–6.

8. Singapore, for example, or Pinochet's Chile, which Harvey describes as "the first experiment with neoliberal state formation" (Harvey, *A Brief History of Neoliberalism*, 7).

9. Hayek, *The Road to Serfdom*, 95; and see Hayek, "The Uses of Knowledge in Society," *American Economic Review* 35, no. 4 (September 1945): 519–30; see also Stedman Jones, *Masters of the Universe*, 59.

10. For discussion on this point, see Stedman Jones, *Masters of the Universe*, 59–60; and Slobodian, *Globalists*, 396.

11. Hayek, *The Road to Serfdom*, 165–66.

12. Hayek, *The Road to Serfdom*, 69, 73, 95, and "Kinds of Order in Society," *New Individualist Review* 3, no. 2 (1964). See also Slobodian, *Globalists*, 224–25.

13. Hayek, *The Road to Serfdom*, 87. As Slobodian puts it, neoliberalism does not treat "self-regulating markets as autonomous entities" but understands quite clearly that "the market does not and cannot take care of itself" (Slobodian, *Globalists*, 2). See also Harvey on the strong role that states play under neoliberalism in defending private property rights and entrepreneurial freedoms (Harvey, *A Brief History of Neoliberalism*, 21, 79).

14. Hayek, *The Road to Serfdom*, 88.

15. Hayek, *The Road to Serfdom*, 85.

16. Slobodian, *Globalists*, 13.

17. Slobodian, *Globalists*, 13. For a good example of how this works in practice see Naomi Klein's discussion of the undoing of local initiatives to cultivate a solar industry in Ontario, Canada (Klein, *This Changes Everything: Capitalism versus the Climate* [New York: Simon and Schuster, 2015], 67–69).

18. Although it is true that neoliberalism challenges traditional forms of state sovereignty in important ways (Harvey, *A Brief History of Neoliberalism*, 3), it also depends on "active national effort[s]" to sustain it (Slobodian, *Globalists*, 255).

19. Friedman, *Capitalism and Freedom*, 2.
20. Megay, "Anti-pluralist Liberalism," 425.
21. Megay, "Anti-pluralist Liberalism," 426.
22. Hayek, *The Road to Serfdom*, 205.
23. Hayek, *The Road to Serfdom*, 207.
24. Hayek, *The Road to Serfdom*, 127.
25. Hayek, *The Road to Serfdom*, 207.
26. Friedman, *Capitalism and Freedom*, 14.
27. Friedman, *Capitalism and Freedom*, 28, 128. As Van Horn and Mirowski put it, corporations were "characterized as passive responders to outside forces" with "the only market actor accused of misusing power" being "the trade union" (Van Horn and Mirowski, "The Rise of the Chicago School of Economics and the Birth of Neoliberalism," in Mirowski and Plehwe, *The Road from Mont Pèlerin*, 155). See also Stedman Jones, who notes that the Chicago School under Friedman "did not recognize" the "problem of corporate monopoly," despite its having been a source of concern for earlier neoliberals (Stedman Jones, *Masters of the Universe*, 342, 7).
28. Friedman, *Capitalism and Freedom*, 15.
29. As Stedman Jones puts it, whereas Hayek had seen "a legitimate role for government in . . . the prevention of private monopolies, and the supervision of natural monopolies," the "members of the second Chicago school such as . . . Milton Friedman" ultimately "reversed the emphasis of early neoliberals on antimonopoly" (Stedman Jones, *Masters of the Universe*, 67; and see 335). See also Van Horn, "Reinventing Monopoly and the Role of Corporations: The Roots of Chicago Law and Economics," in Mirowski and Plehwe, *The Road from Mont Pèlerin*, 204.
30. Hayek, *The Road to Serfdom*, 136.
31. Hayek, *The Road to Serfdom*, 166.
32. Ludwig von Mises, *Bureaucracy* (Indianapolis: Liberty Fund, 1972), 72.
33. Mises, *Bureaucracy*, 8. Hayek also referred to "the sovereignty of the consumer" (Hayek, "The Present State of the Debate," in *Collectivist Economic Planning*, ed. F. A. Hayek [London: Routledge and Kegan Paul, 1935], 241; cited in Slobodian, *Globalists*, 118).
34. Mises, *Bureaucracy*, 72, 17.
35. See, for example, Michel Foucault, *Discipline and Punish: The Birth of the Prisons*, trans. Alan Sheridan (New York: Vintage, 1979).
36. See Elizabeth Anderson, *Private Government: How Employers Rule Our Lives (And Why We Don't Talk about It)* (Princeton, NJ: Princeton University Press, 2017).
37. Rob Nixon, *Slow Violence and the Environmentalism of the Poor* (Cambridge, MA: Harvard University Press, 2011), 107.
38. Nixon, *Slow Violence*, 107. See also Gomez-Barris's discussion of how "military, corporate, and state technologies" work together in "extractive zones," utilizing violence against activists and local Indigenous peoples to advance corporate control and profits (Macarena Gomez-Barris, *The Extractive Zone: Social Ecologies and Decolonial Perspectives* [Durham, NC: Duke University Press, 2017], 196, 33–34, and see xviii and xix).
39. Nixon, *Slow Violence*, 107.
40. Harvey, *A Brief History of Neoliberalism*, 41. See also Brown's discussion of neoliberalism's "remaking of the soul" in *Undoing the Demos*, 22–24, 42–45.
41. Dale W. Jamieson and Marcello Di Paola, "Political Theory for the Anthropocene," chap. 13 in *Global Political Theory*, ed. David Held and Pietro Maffettone (Cambridge: Polity Press, 2016), 267, and see 259–70 for a more general discussion of agency under conditions of neoliberalism.
42. Brown, *Undoing the Demos*, 222.
43. Brown, *Undoing the Demos*, 41. As historians of the movement have shown, "The colonization of new policy pastures with ideas of market liberalization" was a concerted

objective of Chicago School neoliberals (Stedman Jones, *Masters of the Universe*, 92–93, 336).

44. Harvey, *A Brief History of Neoliberalism*, 41.
45. en.oxforddictionaries.com/definition/exploitation.
46. Sharon R. Krause, *Freedom Beyond Sovereignty* (Chicago: University of Chicago Press, 2015), esp. chaps. 4 and 5.
47. John Locke, *Two Treatises of Government*, ed. Peter Laslett (Cambridge: Cambridge University Press, 1988), *Second Treatise*, 283–84.
48. Locke, *Second Treatise*, 382, 398, 400.
49. Locke, *Second Treatise*, 283, 367.
50. Locke, *Second Treatise*, 373.
51. Locke, *Second Treatise*, 367.
52. Locke, *Second Treatise*, 284.
53. Locke, *Second Treatise*, 358.
54. Locke, *Second Treatise*, 353, and see 357.
55. Locke, *Second Treatise*, 377, 359.
56. The rule of law, an institutional separation of powers, and the separation of church and state are also, of course, important mechanisms for constraining power in Locke. We shall explore the separation of powers presently in connection with Montesquieu, who gave the idea fuller development; the other mechanisms are left aside for present purposes.
57. Locke, *Second Treatise*, 362.
58. Locke, *Second Treatise*, 361.
59. Locke, *Second Treatise*, 362.
60. For a rich account of how property rights (and human rights more broadly) have "provided a political justification for the neoliberal counter-revolution of the late twentieth century" and are "mobilized in defense of wealth and power in the period of neoliberal hegemony," see Jessica Whyte, *The Morals of the Market: Human Rights and the Rise of Neoliberalism* (London: Verso, 2019), 3.
61. Although the capture of governments by large-scale economic actors makes the consolidation of economic power dangerous on multiple dimensions, one of which is that arbitrary economic power tends to make government power arbitrary too.
62. Locke, *Second Treatise*, 330.
63. Locke, *Second Treatise*, 328, and see 359.
64. Montesquieu, *The Spirit of the Laws*, trans. Anne M. Cohler, Basia Carolyn Miller, and Harold Samuel Stone (Cambridge: Cambridge University Press, 1989), book XI, chap. 4, p. 155.
65. Montesquieu, *The Spirit of the Laws*, XI.4, 155.
66. Montesquieu, *The Spirit of the Laws*, XI.6, 157.
67. Montesquieu, *The Spirit of the Laws*, II.4, 18.
68. Montesquieu, *The Spirit of the Laws*, XXII.13, 416.
69. Montesquieu, *The Spirit of the Laws*, XXI. 20, 389.
70. Montesquieu, *The Spirit of the Laws*, III.10, 29.
71. Montesquieu, *The Spirit of the Laws*, III.10, 30.
72. Montesquieu, *The Spirit of the Laws*, III.10, 30.
73. Montesquieu, *The Spirit of the Laws*, III.5, 25–26, III.6–7, IV.2.
74. Montesquieu, *The Spirit of the Laws*, IV.2, 33.
75. Montesquieu, *The Spirit of the Laws*, IV.2, 33.
76. Mill insists in his *Principles of Political Economy* that "laisser-faire, in short, should be the general practice; every departure from it, unless required by some great good, is a certain evil" (Mill, *Principles of Political Economy* in *Collected Works of John Stuart Mill*, ed. J. M. Robson, vols. 2–3 [Toronto: University of Toronto Press, 1965], III, 945). As Gerald Gaus points out, however, Mill goes on to elaborate an extensive list of exceptions to this

rule, exceptions that would justify intervention (Gaus, "Mill's Normative Economics," chap. 32 in *A Companion to Mill*, ed. Christopher Macleod and Dale E. Miller [Malden, MA: Blackwell, 2017], 492). See also Jonathan Riley, "Introduction" in John Stuart Mill, *Principles of Political Economy* (Oxford: Oxford University Press, 1994), xli–xlii; cited in Gaus.

77. Jill Gordon shows that the metaphor "does not come from Mill's own text" and "does not reflect accurately Mill's views on free speech expressed in *On Liberty*" (Gordon, "John Stuart Mill and the 'Marketplace of Ideas,'" *Social Theory and Practice* 23, no. 2 [Summer 1997]: 235).

78. John Stuart Mill, *On Liberty*, ed. Elizabeth Rapaport (Indianapolis: Hackett, 1978), 4.

79. Mill, *On Liberty*, 4.

80. Mill, *On Liberty*, 4.

81. Mill, *On Liberty*, 4–5.

82. As Friedman himself also acknowledged, albeit indirectly. He points out that "if economic power is joined to political power, concentration seems almost inevitable. On the other hand, if economic power is kept in separate hands from political power, it can serve as a check and a counter to political power" (Friedman, *Capitalism and Freedom*, 16). Friedman was worried about firms being dominated by government, not the reverse, as in our current situation, but the basic logic is sound. Today this logic reinforces the importance of getting corporate money out of politics and constraining the scale and scope of corporate power.

83. Brown, *Undoing the Demos*, 152–53.

84. J. K. Gibson-Graham, *Postcapitalist Politics* (Minneapolis: University of Minnesota Press, 2006), 62.

85. David Schlosberg and Romand Coles, "The New Environmentalism of Everyday Life: Sustainability, Material Flows, and Movements," in *The Greening of Everyday Life: Challenging Practices, Imagining Possibilities* John M. Meyer and Jens M. Kersten (Oxford: Oxford University Press, 2016), 16.

86. Some of these changes might involve subsidies, but revising regulatory schemes that disadvantage small producers relative to large ones also would be valuable.

87. This paragraph draws from Sharon R. Krause, "Creating a Culture of Environmental Responsibility," chap. 4 in *Cultural Values in Political Economy*, edited by J. P. Singh (Stanford: Stanford University Press, 2020), 65–86.

88. Brown, "Neoliberalism and the End of Liberal Democracy," 6.

89. Whyte, *The Morals of the Market*, 194, 188.

90. Whyte, *The Morals of the Market*, 194.

91. Whyte, *The Morals of the Market*, 3.

92. https://www.supremecourt.gov/opinions/20pdf/20-107_ihdj.pdf.

93. For discussion of neoliberalism's "Wizard of Oz effect" in which "the order projects an ideological mirage of its omnipotence," see Coles, *Visionary Pragmatism*, 119. As Coles points out, there is nothing actually inevitable or irresistible about neoliberalism.

94. Brown, "Neoliberalism and the End of Liberal Democracy," 12–13.

95. Brown, "Neoliberalism and the End of Liberal Democracy," 13.

96. One thing that Hayek got right was to see that "it is not the source but the limitation of power which prevents it from being arbitrary" (*The Road to Serfdom*, 111). Or Hayek got this *partly* right: The source of power does matter to its legitimacy, but it is not the only thing that matters.

97. On the notion of fugitive democracy, see Sheldon Wolin, "Fugitive Democracy" in *Democracy and Difference: Contesting the Boundaries of the Political*, ed. Seyla Benhabib (Princeton, NJ: Princeton University Press, 1996), 31–45.

98. Brown, *Undoing the Demos*, 220.

CHAPTER 2

Uncensorable Speech and the Snares of Illiberalism

Elizabeth S. Anker

One commonplace of the Trump era and its aftermath is that conservatives have "weaponized" the First Amendment and a dedication to free speech historically promoted within many circles of the left.[1] This is a diagnosis offered by Supreme Court Justice Elena Kagan,[2] and it has since headlined seemingly endless op-eds and other referenda addressing the rise of an "illiberal" politics. As Joan Scott puts it: "These days, free speech is the mantra of the right, its weapon in the new culture war."[3] At once, parallel alarm over efforts to turn speech rights into a battleground on college and university campuses has dominated the airwaves. As philosophers Kate Manne and Jason Stanley argue regarding fights over speech on campus, "The notion of freedom of speech is being co-opted by dominant social groups, distorted to serve their interests, and used to silence those who are oppressed and marginalized."[4] One can only expect that such fights over the scope and significance of protected speech will become increasingly polarizing and combative.

    A few things about this rapidly changing terrain governing the conventional fault lines regarding freedom of speech and expression are key. First, that shift marks a quintessential instance of how the extremist right is hijacking a stance often associated with a critical, left, or progressive agenda and politics. Such forms of cooptation have been true of other strongholds of leftist and critical thought, whether manifest in growing conservative skepticism regarding legality or an insistence on constructivist, relativist conceptions of truth. Just as attacks on the rule of law have been a Breitbart platform, it has been trendy to dub the Trump era one of "post-truth." But something more seems to be at issue than a now-standard line of assessment we might trace to Bruno Latour and his caution that "critique has run out of steam."[5] While these developments are clearly part

43

of a larger plundering and transfer of tactics from left to right, debates about free, uncensored speech also illustrate how and why certain justificatory frameworks long adhered to among the left are prone to backfire—and in ways that raise deeper questions about anti-liberal critiques of law broadly. Why can the left appear strangely ill equipped to stave off *il*liberal assertions regarding the uncensorablility of certain speech acts?

Second, these debates raise further questions about the relationship between *anti*-liberalism, *il*-liberalism, and the geopolitical and jurisprudential guises of both liberalism and *neo*liberalism. It has become pro forma for critical theorists to deploy the language of neoliberalism to critique certain faces of law and politics that just as much beg to be labeled *il*liberal. Perhaps above all, the term neoliberalism has been enlisted to protest the capture of political processes by the logic of the market, or the growing recruitment of economizing metrics of analysis to oversee legal principles and jurisprudence. For Wendy Brown, neoliberal rationality has above all presided over the corporatization (and commodification) of speech rights, an outcome epitomized in the *Citizens United* decision.[6] In Brown's thinking, one frequent ploy of neoliberal reason is to promote a free speech platform as a pretext for the economic encroachment on what should remain strictly political spheres of civic life and thought.

A few things about Brown's conceptual geography are telling. To begin, Brown draws on well-established arguments that have historically been recruited to critique liberalism, as her analyses partake of a series of classically *anti-liberal* moves. However, she applies those moves not only to a mix of what she labels *neo*liberalism but also to expose the deceptions of various phenomena increasingly deemed hallmarks of *il*liberalism. In effect, she requisitions an anti-liberal critical arsenal although does so to battle with what are at base alternate if contrasting modes of anti-liberalism. These complex interactions between (neo)liberalism, illiberalism, and anti-liberalism are one site of confusion probed within this essay.

Brown's anti-liberalism also stems from a critical tradition that has long staked its own self-image on a highly specific account of the errors of liberalism (or, today, neoliberalism). In many ways, the intellectual formation of critical theory took shape against the background of distinct historical developments, including regnant ideas about mid-century totalitarianism and theories that understood power to be consolidated by the monopolization of truth and engulfment of pluralistic, dissensual speech. Although this mid-century view of power has frequently united more mainstream liberals and the radical left, critical theorists have rationalized those accounts of power and accompanying emphases on dissensual speech through a chain of oppositions that villainize (neo)liberalism. As a result, critical theory can seem to depend on antithetical ideas about liberalism, projecting onto the liberal tradition a series of features thereby deemed inherently anti-critical (and anti-theoretical): legalism, rationalism, universalism, instrumentalism, reformism, rights-based individualism, and so on.

However, such reasoning hinges on certain slippages. For instance, neoliberalism is cast as a clear outgrowth of classical liberalism, although one that ramps up tendencies imagined to be intrinsic to liberal thought. As we will see, such a genealogy becomes significantly more complicated when debates about free speech are on the table. Severely muddied is not only the unbroken narrative treating neoliberalism as a natural culmination of tendencies implicit to classical liberalism but also other premises underlying most critical theory—in particular, that power gains in strength by preying upon and seeking to censor modes of free, untrammeled discourse and expression.

For reasons that should be clear, the rise of *il*liberalisms that preach an economizing creed of free speech explodes any illusion that anti-censorship or a spirit of "speech-for-speech's sake" are exclusively left-liberal rallying cries. That illusion, I'll suggest, has fulfilled a deeply autobiographical function within many corners of critical theory and Continental thought. A commitment to free speech has been methodologically and ideologically hardwired into many wildly influential schools of theory.

So on the one hand, this lineage suggests why it can be difficult for leftist (e.g., anti-liberal) thinkers to diagnose and in particular to countermand the *il*-liberal appropriation of free speech as a crusade, given how that agenda defies received assumptions about power and its relationship to dissent. But on the other hand, these dynamics raise the question of where that stock equation between a left or progressive politics and a doctrine of anti-censorship came from. One such narrative would emphasize the complicities of the radical left in creating an environment ripe for right-wing takeover. For instance, others have charted how the activism of a figure like Ralph Nader eroded various legal barriers to pave the path to today's expanded protections for corporate speech.[7] But this essay instead investigates the complex of historical-intellectual influences that rendered specifically disorderly, undisciplined free expression an article of faith among a wide congregation of leftist thinkers. Many of those sources are cultural ones, attributable to a mindset popularized by the student protest and countercultural movements of the 1960s. But at the same time, a congeries of other theoretical-methodological preoccupations fused to produce a powerful conceptual-diagnostic matrix that anointed freedom of speech as a particularly sacrosanct right. The bulk of this essay disentangles those multiple influences, studying the ways they became interwoven and self-corroborating. I'll therefore wrestle with a sequence of default assumptions that have shaped substantial theoretical and critical work on law: among others, that rules are constituted through their exceptions, that lending expression to marginalized and censored perspectives is a failsafe strategy of critique, and more.

The side effects of this valorization of unrestricted speech, however, are another matter. Doctrinal investment in free expression exacerbates a chronic line-drawing problem—regarding speech and more—within the left. The definitions of speech undergirding most (if not all) theoretical positions have tended either to bracket and/or evacuate speech of its content or to imagine unrestricted speech to be intrinsically justice-producing, plurivocal, and self-complicating—in reasoning that jettisons matters of substance and content. There are, of course, good reasons for this reluctance to impose positivistic, normative, or authoritative criteria on speech, which I'll historicize, attributing them above all to a Cold War climate of rising fears about totalitarianism and instrumental reason. However, the historical specificity of that climate also provokes debates about whether the unique crises that initially germinated such fears have not been superseded, revealing a privileging of open-ended, self-pluralizing speech to be a relic of a bygone era.

Irony and the Left

There is little question that the spirit of 1968 left an indelible imprint on left, progressive intellectual life. While one might dispute the hues and gradations of that watermark, it instilled within leftist thought and especially critical theory a deep commitment to freedom of expression. We can quickly grasp how both the student protest and countercultural movements were erected upon a generalized faith in the emancipatory (and, conversely, potentially oppressive) capacities of language—a faith that academic theory happily adopted, carving it into stone. A retrospective study like Marshall Berman's 1982 *All That Is Solid Melts into Air: The Experience of Modernity* sums up many aspects of that spirit, and in terms that academic theory assembled into a highly specific model of what anti-authoritarian expression should entail. Overall, Berman explains the 1960s as a saga of waning hope in the synthesis promised by the dialectic, as he explains how the left in that decade's aftermath metabolized a sense of omnipresent contradiction that, however, would not be quelled by resolution or transcendence.[8] Yet for Berman, this dialecticism without reprieve is far from disabling; quite differently, it allowed a particular flavor of Romantic moderni*sm* (for instance, associated by Berman with Baudelaire) to emerge triumphant.

Different aspects of Berman's vision of "modernism in the streets" distill other commonly held expectations that helped to transform self-pluralizing freedom of expression into its own left intellectual nostrum. To begin, Berman explicitly understands that ethos in terms of a recurring style or voice—a voice, for instance, linking Nietzsche with Marx. As Berman explains of such a style, it "resonates at once with self-discovery and self-mockery, with self-delight and self-doubt. . . . It is ironic and contradictory, polyphonic and dialectical," involving "rhythms" and "range."[9] Beyond a thematic emphasis on the voice, this appeal to style and genre, first, delineates radicalism in terms of a privileging of the *form* of representation over its subject matter and content. Second, Berman's nod to "self-discovery" evokes the broad ethos of consciousness-raising that animated student protest and the counterculture—and that survives in a range of contemporary theoretical axioms. Relatedly, and third, we should note Berman's language of the "polyphonic" or plurivocal—as opposed to speech characterized as coherent, universalizable, stable, or unitary.

Yet of perhaps greatest importance is Berman's allusion to "irony," a term that reverberates throughout his study. As he surmises of the "self-divisions" produced within the left (due, among other factors, to a failure of dialectical synthesis): "So long as we grasped our self-divisions, they infused the New Left with a deep sense of irony, a tragic irony that haunted all our spectacular productions of political comedy."[10] This tribute to irony and comedy is another signature of much critical theory today, even while that emphasis took hold during Berman's period of the 1980s and 1990s. For Berman and many others, that ironic mode has equaled a highly specific kind of speech: speech not only rife with internal dissensions (or dialecticism) but that actively leverages those ambiguities.

We can look to another influential spokesperson for "irony," Richard Rorty, for a fuller picture of this broad temper. Even while Rorty (a proponent of his own odd variant of liberalism) represents something of an intellectual outlier, his expectations for irony have been part of a mindset that remains a theoretical mainstay. As for Berman, Rorty's paean to irony, his 1989 *Contingency, Irony, Solidarity*, feeds into a theory of "pluralism" that Rorty advances as the recipe for democratic tolerance. Rorty locates his version of liberal plurality within the "radical diversity of private purposes, of the radically poetic character of individual lives, and of the merely poetic foundations of the 'we-consciousness' which lies behind our social institutions."[11] Also like Berman, Rorty's dialectic is a notably dematerialized one, which he construes as "the attempt to play off vocabularies against one another."[12] In his reasoning, irony therefore possesses both critical and transformative faculties. Just as it entails the "opposite of . . . common sense," Rorty lauds the "marginalized," "idiosyncratic," "unfamiliar" character of the awareness effectuated by attention to irony.[13] Although couched in the language of liberalism, Rorty's focus on the ways irony can work to contest the status quo (or, for Rorty, "a lot of stodgy literal talk") marshals a widely subscribed to conception of political engagement.[14]

Such a politics of irony is also predicated on belief in the incredible force of the symbolic: of words, language, and representations to constitute and alter reality, for better and for worse. For many theorists working within the humanities over past decades, it has been standard to thus conceive of politics as a battle over competing representations. By many accounts, that emphasis on the symbolic was also championed by 1960s radicals who lauded "cultural struggle" and theaters of reimagination for possessing a higher political authority and ground.[15] As Sean McCann and Michael Szalay argue, the consciousness-raising orientation of such a politics naturalized not only the "idea that performance itself functions as a kind of therapeutic rite aimed at the self-realization of its participants" but also a cult of risk and magic.[16] Perhaps above all was such a project of "freeing one's mind" a carnival of undisciplined, unforeseeable, anti-authoritarian speech and free expression. So the peculiar flavor of 1960s protest and of the counterculture gives us one set of explanations for why a faith in uncensorable speech became a calling card of the radical left.

In a well-known story, these priorities were rechanneled into academic theory, as the vestiges of 1960s-style insurrection were housed and thereafter domesticated within the Anglo-American university, given new life in particular in language and literature departments. But while lending intellectual backing to the exuberant experimentalism of the 1960s, the theory era simultaneously generated a series of overlapping frameworks that consecrated speech-for-speech's sake as an unqualified ideal. While exalting a theatrics of the symbolic, the intellectual left associated with theory also increasingly promoted theories of power that understand its operations to be foremost discursive and representational. One version of such thinking can be attributed to Foucault, who conceives of modern disciplinary power as multiplying its capillary effects through a web of interlocking discourses and regimes of institutional expertise. Yet at the same time, leftist thinkers have emphasized the violence perpetrated by language, both as an archive of history's abuses but also as the scaffolding of structural and other oppression. It has been prevailing wisdom that domination is secured by representations—although totalizing, colonizing, censoring, repressive ones. As Audre Lorde would therefore famously caution in 1984: "The master's tools will never dismantle the master's house."

But it took what is often dubbed the "linguistic turn" (and especially post-Saussurian linguistics) to fashion and incorporate this prioritization of undisciplined discourse into a full-fledged theory of semiotics. This body of predominantly deconstructive theory (whether of Judith Butler or Jacques Derrida or Paul de Man) has promoted its own spirit of infinite dialecticism without unification or resolution, not so far afield from the sort proselytized by Berman. Whether foremost associated with deconstruction, psychoanalysis, or the other variants of poststructuralism overseeing progressive legal thought, a set of core premises concerning language and speech were instilled to become academic second nature.

One involves the view that *all* representations will somehow be embedded within chains of supplementarity and therefore fail to be self-sufficient or stable, instead caught up in their own residues, aporias, and failures. On the one hand, this renders language itself fundamentally ungovernable, unpredictable, and indeterminate. But on the other, it has meant that any speech act is paradoxically both enabled and imperiled by its misprisions and other remainders. For some, this representational economy has imbued such difference and Otherness internal to discourse with a certain mystique or allure (and even ethics), just as those resistances have been heralded as bottomlessly fertile and productive. But what results is that a separate rationale for prizing uncensorable and free speech stems from post-Saussurian theories of language—which plain and simply mandate that priority. Conversely, this thinking has meant that efforts to control or regulate speech have been treated as blatantly wrong.

That framework generates its own rationales for lauding such uncensorable speech precisely due to its refusal of content. Much as post-Saussurian semiotics locates preeminent meaning with the gaps and deferrals of language—or within failures of perfect correspondence and objectivizable knowing—so, too, has political speech been valued accordingly. Hence, the speech touted as uncensorable by many theorists has been viewed as insurrectionary due to more than its supposed politics: its insurrectionary status also lies with its refusal of normative, substantive truth content and bearings. However, that emphasis on the productively anti-normative inarticulacy of certain speech acts is exactly what has proven self-sabotaging with the rise of illiberalism. In other words, this legacy of Saussure—or the conceit that speech defiant of censorship will also be self-emptying of objectivizable or positive content—works to deprive theorists of an evaluative mechanism for assessing when a given speech act should versus should not be subject to legal or other regulation.

Exceptionalizing the Law

Thus far, this essay has dealt in somewhat more abstract philosophical notions that rendered anti-censorship a cardinal principle within many camps of critical theory and leftist thought. Yet those assumptions were forged amid highly specific political-intellectual and historical crucibles. A countercultural romance of insurrectionary speech was married to multiple other warrants for thus prioritizing language resistant to censorship, warrants that also helped to integrate such reasoning into critical *legal* thought and specifically legal questions. Critiques of law, for instance, have regularly relied on the exact tenets I've just outlined, even when those critiques set out to advance normative agendas. This relative agreement within the left legal academe over the value of specifically marginalized speech is striking given the extent to which it reveals scholarship firmly situated within law schools to be beholden to the same assumptions that have overtaken language, literature, and other humanities fields.

Across the university, much critical scholarship has been motivated by the imperative to lend speech and expression to society's oppressed, or to those perspectives historically silenced by law and other organs of power. One of the most visible and recurring critiques of law has accordingly been that the legal system has actively enforced the censorship of certain lives and voices. Intersectionality theory of the sort pioneered by Kimberle Crenshaw, for instance, was launched in order to remedy the "problems of exclusion" resulting from not only law's censoring operations but also parallel occlusions within both CLS thought and feminist jurisprudence.[17] As Crenshaw complains, the universal womanhood evoked by "second wave" (and predominantly white) feminists only compounds Black women's longstanding ostracism.[18] For Crenshaw, recuperating the "voices" unwittingly censored by feminism is therefore one key avenue to expanding the law's scope of representation to include Black women's experiences.

But at the same time, those suppressed viewpoints have been celebrated for additional reasons—namely, because they promise to usher in forms of heightened awareness and understanding. In such reasoning, the recovery of censored speech works not only to critique law for its omissions but also to consciousness-raise and even to transform. Working within critical race theory, a thinker like Mari Matsuda notably cites W. E. B. Du Bois for such a sensibility. Updating Du Bois's emphasis on duality, Matsuda avers that a "multiple consciousness" will elicit privileged epistemic truths, given how "the victims of oppression have distinct normative insights."[19] For Matsuda, "adopting the perspective of those who have seen and felt the falsity of the liberal promise" can thus enable a reimagining of the relation between law and justice.[20] But, for Matsuda, those perspectives will lead to more than the exposure and reversal of law's historical bastions of censorship. Rather, Matsuda also extols the "transformative skill" over language (citing Henry Louis Gates) engendered by the experiences of self-division remarked upon by Du Bois.[21] In such thinking, structures of silencing (political and symbolic) exist as more than limits or errors to be corrected. That censored speech also comes to be valorized in its own right as procuring superior, more ethical, and just ways of knowing.

These sorts of emphases have been so widespread as to connect groundbreaking legal theorists of race like Matsuda and Crenshaw with a comparatively revolutionary thinker as Judith Butler. Butler's 1990 *Gender Trouble* mobilizes near-identical premises, despite that text's many differences with legal scholarship. *Gender Trouble* opens with its own series of rebukes of feminism for being fundamentally censoring. As Butler similarly alleges, feminism relies on a unitary and stable conception of womanhood, enforcing "coercive and regulatory" conformity to those dominant norms.[22] Butler's project in developing a genealogy of gender, in contrast, endeavors to lay bare those "exclusionary practices" that would otherwise remain concealed (5). Butler's theory of course derives from a blend of Lacanian psychoanalysis, with a deconstructive semiotics, with an account of discourse-as-power imbibed from Foucault. But at the heart of Butler's charges against feminism is the complaint that it subscribes to a simplistically mimetic, essentializing, and in consequence censoring theory of representation, linguistic and political. Feminists, in effect, naïvely bought into a misguided understanding of how language works. Whereas for Butler, *all* identities (being mere representations) are constructed in discourse and, beyond being artificial, are haunted by the infinite remainders that supplement them: in other words, by the truths that they silence. Butler also gives us another rationale for recouping this syndrome as far from wholly negative but instead strangely productive: she develops those recognitions into a theory of agency as performative re-signification.

This emphasis on those truths invariably censored by any norm or dominant—and corollary expectation that such perspectives will harbor privileged understanding—has found separate justification in political theology. In assessing the points of overlap between left versus right variants of anti-liberalism, political theology is clearly key. It has provided a hugely important conduit for and framework for articulating the anti-liberalism (or irrationalism) of critical and leftist thought—just as it is core to the *il*liberalisms now promoted by thinkers like Adrian Vermeule. Whereas political theology generates independent rationales for valorizing the anti-rationalist and decisionist character of legal decision-making (e.g., sovereignty), it similarly confirms the view that crucial recognitions regarding law and legality are found in the exceptions to law-on-the-books—or that are censored within law's official corpus.

One such source of political theology has been Robert Cover's thought. While perhaps best known for his reflections on the violence that haunts "even the most routine of legal acts," Cover also insists on the importance of exceptional or seemingly rare cases. Apparent outliers like death penalty judgments and expressions of martyrdom are for Cover crucial to comprehending the ordinary workings of law, including their philosophical implications.[23]

Even more formidable an influence than Cover has been Carl Schmitt's theory. For Schmitt, the exceptional case not only possesses "decisive meaning which exposes the core of the matter," or a kind of heightened revelatory capacity.[24] In addition, Schmitt hallows the exception as fully necessary to consolidate the norm, in a paradoxical relay. Even while it "defies general codification," Schmitt's exception is "not peripheral but essential" to the legal rule's sheer existence as well as feint of naturalness.[25] All norms, once again, will depend on their exceptions: on what they censor and suppress. Yet beyond being submerged, those censored truths are fundamentally resistant to legal articulation—in short, defiant of any attempt to rectify their condition of censorship. As such, thinkers like Schmitt and Cover offer another basis for venerating censored and excluded truths, given that they are pregnant with preeminent insight into the law's overarching structure. Impossible to codify, the exception for Schmitt is here again generatively mobile, liminal, and fleeting—fundamentally eluding stabilizing, positivistic, mimetic orders of representation. When transferred to debates about speech, we can grasp how and why such reasoning would further contribute to a reluctance to codify the content or substance of those censored or exceptional truths, since any such attempt would divest them of their revelatory promise. One core point of work like Schmitt's thus lies with the impossibility of stipulating the exception's insurgent, antinomian content in any rationalist or objective grammar: a liberal project that Schmitt presents as fully dangerous.

Censorship, the Cold War, and Radical Democracy

These sorts of premises assumed their contours against the backdrop of the Cold War and the preoccupation with censorship it understandably fomented for thinkers of all stripes. That fixation on the perils of Cold War censorship importantly dovetailed with and reinforced the assumptions about the censoring effects of any given dominant considered above. The spectralization of political censorship (whether behind the Iron Curtain or within apartheid South Africa) independently confirmed the paramount onus to protect and to recover silenced, suppressed, ostracized speech—although, internationally, the encroachments of totalitarianism (versus liberal legalistic rationalism) were taken as the main threat jeopardizing plurivocal speech of all kinds. But that shadow of totalitarianism imbued a focus on freedom of speech and expression with additional meanings we have yet to consider.

One staple of many theorizations of totalitarianism is that freedom of speech functions as a sort of threshold right that, if violated, will precipitate a cascade of other rights infringements. Conversely, totalitarianism has often been defined as a political form fully motored by the impetus to prey upon speech. These dynamics expected to accompany totalitarian power created further justifications for hallowing the uncensorable voice at all costs—and, once again, for its own sake, irrespective of substance or content. Whereas speech has been touted as the core of the human (and of humanism), many efforts by literary and other theorists to reckon with violence, pain, and suffering have separately trained attention on the deleterious effects—political and symbolic—of endangered or abrogated speech. Taken as a whole, this body of work has often trumpeted speech rights as barrier or stopgap fending off the many dangers posed by Cold War politics.

Elaine Scarry's path-breaking 1985 work *The Body in Pain* exemplifies the sort of thinking that helped to disseminate and to naturalize such a logic: thinking that is also central to first generation (i.e., Yale School) trauma theory. While Scarry's study is nominally a phenomenology of pain, those effects are simultaneously held out as lessons in power's anatomy—which for Scarry actualizes itself by attacking the voice. Scarry's seminal insights into pain—that it is "unshareable" and "world-destroying"—therefore carry decidedly political stakes, just as her book's opening chapters on torture and war probe the representational hurdles faced by organizations like Amnesty International (winner of the 1977 Amnesty International Peace Prize).[26] Beyond those themes, a few aspects of Scarry's study are key. To begin, Scarry defines power, given how it induces pain and lays siege to the voice, in terms of a fundamentally totalitarian relationship to language. As she explains, torture first "monopolizes language, becom[ing] its only subject" (54) and thereafter enacts "the conversion of absolute pain into the fiction of absolute power" (27). Just as important, it is when speech fails to communicate that its content becomes liable to appropriation to shore up even "debased" forms of power.[27] *The Body in Pain* thereby ratifies a then-growing left wisdom that power is aggrandized by censoring, exiling, and dominating certain voices, along with the corollary that resistance to power begins with the rescue of such forbidden speech. Clearly, this notion that power obliterates language as a stepping stone to wider assaults upon other freedoms furnishes another set of warrants for enshrining freedom of expression as independently valuable.

In addition, Scarry's premise that pain shatters language exemplifies other reasons that specifically contentless speech has been valorized a stave against the machinations of power. Because when one imagines the task of recovering speech destroyed by experiences of pain, that recovered language would presumably have been reduced, at some point, to a state of incoherence and incomprehensibility. Some theorists of trauma have reveled in that inarticulacy. Yet this pursuit of speech trampled into a condition of unshareability crafts still another basis for protecting speech rights that has little if anything to do with the truth content or normative fiber of that underlying speech—more accurately, hallowing its very unintelligibility. The speech wracked by experiences of trauma and pain is explained as, by definition, evacuated of evidentiary and other positivistic value. But insofar as the fate of speech under torture functions as a microcosm of totalitarian power, that tangled relation endows such speech with a privileged authority precisely because it has been fractured and rendered incommunicable.

Many theorists of radical democracy have echoed these basic axioms and assumptions about the inherently resistant status of free, open-ended discourse, lauding undisciplined speech as crucial to forging a democratic culture. Radical democratic theory largely came of age through a sequence of attempts to reckon with the nature of specifically mid-century, Cold War expressions of authoritarianism. In so doing, it has defined democracy by erecting totalitarianism into its antithesis and foil (much like the status of neoliberalism assumes for theorists still today). Central to that explanatory matrix is the conceit that those political forms could be differentiated through their competing stances or attitudes toward the fundamentally ungrounded category of the "People." While of a twentieth-century vintage, that tradition of theorizing democracy endows such a conception of democracy's People with a lineage typically traced to Rousseau. As Etienne Balibar puts it, Rousseau was the first to pose the question, "What makes a people a people?"[28] and thereby to recognize that such a category would inherently unstable and indeterminate. As Rousseau is understood to have first fully grasped, democracy is constituted by a fictitious positing of the preexistence of a People, even while that gesture retroactively (and performatively) brings that category into being.[29] Like other nonmimetic representations, this lack of secure foundations underlying democracy has been seen both to threaten and to enable its practice, for instance rendering any representation of the People fertilely open-ended.

Theorists during the Cold War returned to Rousseau's reflections to place them in a mid-century light. Among other things, those mid-century spins on Rousseau emphasize the modes of political speech that totalitarianism is unable to tolerate—here, too, prizing speech animated by its own indeterminacy. Whereas political evil is conceived in terms of hostility to such centrifugal speech, theorists simultaneously influenced by the linguistic turn instead foreground the proto-linguistic dimensions of democratic practice. For example, Claude Lefort's thought is illuminating, given how he patterns the interrelated categories of the People, democracy, and the political on a semiotics derived from Lacan. Lefort's reasoning generalizes the sorts of recognitions one might attribute to Rousseau onto *all* nonmimetic representations, conceiving the dilemmas of specifically political "representation" vis-à-vis a theory of language predicated on the impossibility of stable or complete reference. Just as the People's "identity" will be elusive, so, too, will all symbolizations of the political necessarily—and productively—fail. Democracy is thus presented by Lefort as a type of indeterminate and contentless representation that is nevertheless generatively motored by those very irresolutions and gaps.[30] And it is precisely by keeping alive this play of randomness that politics can elude nefarious attempts to totalize its operations. However, one frequent corollary of reasoning like Lefort's is to insist on the substantive "emptiness" of such language, eschewing matters of truth content and veracity. Speech is accordingly deemed democratic or "political" based on its very indeterminacy.

Let me briefly engage one other thinker with substantial contemporary influence to further comprehend how this conceptual matrix has contributed to a valorization of speech-for-speech's sake. Important to note as before are the variety of intellectual influences that conspire to reinforce such unbridled faith in the saving powers of aleatory language. In accounting for radical democracy, Chantal Mouffe relies primarily on Schmitt, although to arrive at a position reminiscent of what we've just observed. Like Lefort, Mouffe's 2000 book *The Democratic Paradox* underscores the "representative" and "symbolic" nature of politics, along with the "originary exclusions" in the category of the People that paradoxically facilitate and thereby work to legitimize democracy.[31]

Mouffe is mostly interested in countermanding rationalist philosophies of politics and law, and it is Schmitt's decisionism that Mouffe enlists to capture those hazards of rationalism. Mouffe, like many others, looks to Schmitt's notions of the "exception" and friend-enemy distinction to elucidate that inherent irrationalism—or "antagonism"—thus deemed constitutive of politics. That said, those features are far from lethal for Mouffe, who instead celebrates such anti-rationalism (and, by extension, anti-liberalism) as the lifeblood of democracy. Exalting the "contingent and temporary" status of the People, Mouffe heralds that ephemerality as "the real strength of liberal democracy."[32] What is striking about Mouffe's thinking, especially when juxtaposed with Lefort, is how the backdrop required to offset the contours of democracy migrates from totalitarianism to liberal rationalism. Whereas for mid-century thinkers like Lefort the totalitarian understandably loomed large, for Mouffe rationalism becomes the main scourge. But the explanations these thinkers propose for why those guises of power possess predatory appetites are interchangeable if not identical. The anti-democratic orientations of both liberalism and totalitarianism are imagined to stifle and domineer the plurivocal—or indeterminate, diffuse speech. As Mouffe puts it, rationalism tries to eliminate and master that "undecidability" precisely by imposing a "univocal model" of decision-making.[33]

Less worrisome within the context of this essay is the symmetry that folds ideas about totalitarianism and rationalism into a single theory of power. Yet what such reasoning further does is to conceive *il*liberalism of the sort manifest *both* in fascism (e.g., Schmitt) *and* liberal rationalism (e.g., neoliberalism) in terms of a mutual if not self-same relationship to speech. One need only click on the *New York Times* or social media for evidence that such an equation between power and univocal discourse is no longer operative. It is more accurate to say that illiberal speech capitalizes on the very dissensus long championed by critical theorists. Just as democracy is deceptively presented as a pageantry of insurrectionary speech, such formulations of politics hinge on reductive, monochromatic, and overly tidy assumptions about democracy's mortal enemies, whether the Cold War or neoliberalism today.

Illiberal Speech

Bruno Latour's 2004 *Critical Inquiry* essay, "Has Critique Run out of Steam? From Matters of Fact to Matters of Concern," inaugurated a line of self-questioning among some theorists that, in Latour's words, has brought "the sword of criticism to criticism itself."[34] As Latour argues, many tried-and-true methodologies long espoused by the critical left have been either coopted or otherwise warped to fulfill a conservative agenda. Latour singles out "critique" and constructivist versions of truth and facts as in particular lending themselves to such opportunism, a syndrome for Latour exemplified in climate change denialism. Part of Latour's project in raising fears about the murky politics of critique is instead to promote activities like "gathering," "assembling," and acknowledging what we "cherish." Yet just as central to that intervention is a plea to "retest the linkages between the new threats" on the sociopolitical horizon and our habituated modes of response: to update and refine our critical strategies to better address the unique political and other crises of the present. If "critique has run out of steam," that is partly because we confront a radically different sociopolitical landscape than the one that gestated the arsenal of critique many decades ago.

In light of the territory this essay has surveyed, Latour's worries about cooptation are striking. Left thinkers in the 1980s and 1990s were alarmed by the prospect that certain left or progressive ideals and agendas like rights were inordinately liable to a (neo)liberal or right-wing takeover that would deplete or pervert their potentially emancipatory promise. And while a heightened risk for utopian legal-political principles such as rights, certain modes of *discourse* were similarly believed to invite usurpation. Above all, arguments couched in clarity, objectivity, transparency, and reason were viewed as liable to being thus hijacked. As Duncan Kennedy thus surmises, "What I think we need to do is look for ways of talking, ways of responding, ways of doing things in which the goal is not to convince people by lucidity.... But rather to operate in the interspace of artifacts, gestures, speech and rhetoric, histrionics, drama."[35] Along with such an ironic discursive register, an emphasis on style was frequently understood as a recipe for avoiding such a fate. Modes of discourse aimed at dialecticism, ambiguity, difficulty, parody, and irony have therefore been extolled for containing built-in mechanisms geared to short circuit conservative attempts to plunder or capture their arguments as well as animating principles. At the heart of that privileging of certain resistant genres of activism and protest has been conviction in the insurrectionary potential of pluralistic, plurivocal modalities of discourse. Speech deemed disorderly, undisciplined, uncensorable, aleatory, and even inarticulate has accordingly been promoted as a bulwark against power and its encroachments. One theoretical maxim is that freedom of expression is necessary to armor a progressive politics—ensuring critical thought's simultaneously anti-totalitarian and anti-liberal fiber.

However, we do not need arguments like Latour's to demonstrate the obsolescence of this conceit that distinctive analytic-rhetorical-stylistic genres will provide an insurance policy against the illiberal use and application of theory, politics, or what might appear a progressive agenda. In fact, it is the dedication to insurrectionary speech long uniting many among the left that is proving especially susceptible to conservative pillaging. Put differently, what if the modes of antinomian, indeterminate speech often touted by theorists, rather than guarding a left or progressive politics against embezzlement, have served to hasten such an outcome? Indeed, illiberalism actively thrives upon and proliferates the exact genres of speech long heralded as inherently anti-fascist and anti-(neo)liberal. So in a "post-truth era," Latour's hobbyhorse of facts denialism may still exemplify such misappropriation of constructivist and relativist theories of meaning and of representation. But it is also true that many architects of *il*liberalism—both within the legal academy and on the judicial bench—have been ardent students not only of Schmitt but also of Foucault. This raises still further questions about the strategic, intentional nature of a right-wing plundering of leftist tactics, making that theft look far from accidental or random.

These intellectual debts and genealogies are troubling for additional reasons than those cited by Latour. Indeed, it is one thing to caution that certain rhetorical-argumentative moves and devices lend themselves to cooptation. However, it is another to raise concerns about whether or not an *il*liberal worldview lurks within the annals of theory: that not only Schmitt but even Foucault's oeuvre contains elements that bear the seeds of authoritarianism and an apologetics for illiberalism. What if the archive of theory is less antiseptically leftist or progressive than we would like to think? Schmitt's legacy is of course an easy target. But what if Foucault and Derrida and Lacan are unacknowledged handmaidens to (if not progenitors of) illiberalism's rise?

This essay has argued that debates about speech visibly blur such divisions—divisions long believed to be set in stone. While the slippery character of arguments defending unrestricted corporate speech are on the one hand historically specific, on the other they mobilize assumptions that are nothing new. In so doing, these debates show us why an emphasis on the uncensorability of certain performative speech acts engrains an emphasis on form and style that has long confronted critical theorists with a line-drawing problem, even while that difficulty becomes especially glaring when restrictions governing speech are under scrutiny. Seeing as free, uncensorable expression has been embraced precisely as a framework for liquidating matters of normative substance and content, it is not surprising that such a basis for barring the regulation of speech would be attractive to authoritarian, illiberal factions on the right.

We could look briefly to a few examples from contemporary politics to illustrate the cunning with which illiberalism commandeers arguments long marshaled by the progressive left. For instance, illiberal speech indeed harnesses a commitment to anti-censorship, although it charges regimes of "identity politics" and "political correctness" (e.g., the discourse of "snowflakes") with wrongly enforcing such discursive policing. Right-wing social movements have simultaneously conscripted a certain faith in the consciousness-raising thrust of claims to inhabit and give voice to socially marginalized and censored positions. Crusaders like those for "men's rights" activate conservative voters by purporting to awaken white men to the terms of their own silencing, although at the hands of "liberal identity politics." These movements deploy a familiar strategy of decrying false consciousness, although to accuse the left establishment of duping men into forfeiting their entitlements.

Yet perhaps most distressing is the frequent genre or style of *il*liberal politics, with its pervasive and unrelenting irony and subversion. Leaving nothing sacred, the authoritarian leanings of the Trump White House were notorious for orchestrating a morass of post-truths, actively setting out to produce a smokescreen of unverifiability. In a kind of plurivocality gone haywire, it is illiberal political speech today that mobilizes what Rorty would call an army of warring metaphors, depriving public discourse of anything resembling a stable ground.[36] Needless to say, this constant barrage of self-canceling position statements also normalizes a culture of distraction that can deprive principled critique of a fixed standpoint or orientation.

We can return to the historical milieu that installed a romance of speech-for-speech's-sake within many corners of the intellectual left to gain still additional insight into the reasons why that doctrine can seem passé. That doctrine, we've seen, was fashioned in response to a particular conception of the anatomy of especially totalitarian-authoritarian power during the Cold War, even while that account of power has been transported to decipher the makeup of liberal-legalistic-rationalism. Such thinking understands power to shore itself up by monopolizing truth and, by extension, speech: by totalizing language and thought. Control and centralization of the symbolic-linguistic has thus been explained as a necessary predicate, or stepping stone, to power—perhaps not surprising in a body of thought governed by post-Saussurian ideas about language.

But we need not look far for evidence that illiberalism today operates quite differently. Within twenty-first-century illiberalism, power more accurately secures itself not through a monolithic guise of truth but rather with cries of "fake news." It defamiliarizes, demystifies, and erodes stability in order to fortify its odd legitimacy. It fans the flames of paranoia and suspicion (for instance, with anti-immigrant sentiment) in order to rationalize its dirty business. It thrives on a combustible mix of indeterminacy, insubstantiality, and foundationless-ness—in other words, on the very liminality that critical theorists have celebrated as intrinsically democratic. In effect, illiberalism breeds the exact conditions of dizzying plurivocality that many progressive thinkers have trumpeted as failsafe checks and balances on power's aggrandizement. Whereas earlier generations of thinkers acclaimed free, unregulated speech as a vital barricade against authoritarianism, it is hard to imagine how such an ethos could begin to counteract the breakdown of public discourse that represents illiberalism's chosen stomping ground today.

Notes

1. It is worth noting that "weaponize" has itself become something of a "word of the year."
2. Adam Liptak, "How Conservatives Weaponized the First Amendment," *New York Times*, June 30, 2018, https://www.nytimes.com/2018/06/30/us/politics/first-amendment-conservatives-supreme-court.html, accessed April 22, 2019. See also Jedediah Purdy, "The Bosses' Constitution," *The Nation*, September 12, 2018.
3. Joan W. Scott, "How the Right Weaponized Free Speech," *Chronicle of Higher Education*, January 7, 2018.
4. Kate Manne and Jason Stanley, "When Free Speech Becomes a Political Weapon," *Chronicle Review*, November 13, 2015.
5. Bruno Latour, "Has Critique Run Out of Steam? From Matters of Fact to Matters of Concern," *Critical Inquiry* 30, no. 2 (Winter 2004): 225–48.
6. Wendy Brown, *Undoing the Demos* (New York: Zone, 2017).
7. See Liptak, "How Conservatives Weaponized the First Amendment."
8. Marshall Berman, *All That Is Solid Melts into Air: The Experience of Modernity* (1982; New York: Penguin, 1988), 329–30.

9. Berman, *All That Is Solid*, 23.
10. Berman, *All That Is Solid*, 328.
11. Richard Rorty, *Contingency, Irony, Solidarity* (Cambridge: Cambridge University Press, 1989), 67.
12. Rorty, *Contingency, Irony, Solidarity*, 78.
13. Rorty, *Contingency, Irony, Solidarity*, 41, 74.
14. Rorty, *Contingency, Irony, Solidarity*, 42.
15. See Sean McCann and Michael Szalay, "Do You Believe in Magic? Literary Thinking after the New Left," *Yale Journal of Criticism* 18, no. 2 (2005): 435–68, 440.
16. McCann and Szalay, "Do You Believe in Magic?," 444.
17. See Kimberle Crenshaw, "Demarginalizing the Intersection of Race and Sex: A Black Feminist Critique of Antidiscrimination Doctrine, Feminist Theory and Antiracist Politics," *University of Chicago Legal Forum* 139 (1989): 139–67, 140. For Crenshaw, the predicament of women of color involves how "their exclusion is reinforced when *white* women speak for and as *women*. The authoritative universal voice—usually white male subjectivity masquerading as non-racial, non-gendered objectivity—is merely transferred to those women, but for gender, share many of the same cultural, economic and social characteristics" (154).
18. Crenshaw, "Demarginalizing the Intersection of Race and Sex," 153.
19. Mari Matsuda, "Looking to the Bottom: Critical Legal Studies and Reparations," 326.
20. Matsuda, "Looking to the Bottom," 324.
21. Matsuda, "Looking to the Bottom," 335.
22. Judith Butler, *Gender Trouble* (New York: Routledge, 1990), 7.
23. *Narrative, Violence, and the Law: The Essays of Robert Cover*, ed. Marth Minow, Michael Ryan, and Austin Sarat (Ann Arbor: University of Michigan Press, 1995), 236, 210. Also like Schmitt, Cover's reckoning with the violence implicit to law extended from his anxieties about the dangers of the overly mechanistic or rationalistic application of legal rules, which he also saw as a symptom of legal positivism as well as liberalism.
24. Carl Schmitt, *The Concept of the Political*, trans. George Schwab (Chicago: University of Chicago Press, 2007), 35.
25. Carl Schmitt, *Political Theology: Four Chapters on the Concept of Sovereignty*, trans. George Schwab (Chicago: University of Chicago Press, 2005), 13; Schmitt, *The Concept of the Political*, 50–51.
26. Elaine Scarry, *The Body in Pain: The Making and Unmaking of the World* (New York: Oxford University Press, 1985), 29.
27. Scarry, *The Body in Pain*, 14.
28. Balibar, *We, the People of Europe? Reflections on Transnational Citizenship*, trans. James Swenson (Princeton, NJ: Princeton, 2003), 94.
29. Rousseau, *The Social Contract and Other Later Political Writings*, ed. Victor Gourevitch (New York: Cambridge, 1997), 71.
30. As an analogue, see, for instance, Paul de Man, "The Resistance to Theory," *Yale French Studies* 63 (1982): 3–20.
31. Chantal Mouffe, *The Democratic Paradox* (Brooklyn: Verso, 2000), 1.
32. Mouffe, *The Democratic Paradox*, 9, 10.
33. Mouffe, *The Democratic Paradox*, 34.
34. Latour, "Has Critique Run Out of Steam?," 227.
35. See Peter Gabel and Duncan Kennedy, "Roll Over Beethoven," *Stanford Law Review* 36, no. 1 (January 1984): 1–55, 9.
36. Nietzsche described truth as a "mobile army of metaphors."

CHAPTER 3

Illiberalism and Administrative Government

Jeremy Kessler

Driven by the perception that liberal democracy is in a state of crisis across the developed world, political and legal commentators have taken to contrasting two alternatives: "illiberal democracy" (or populism) and "undemocratic liberalism" (or technocracy).[1] According to the logic of this antinomy, once an erstwhile liberal-democratic nation-state becomes too populist, it is on the path toward illiberal democracy; once it becomes too technocratic, it is on the path toward undemocratic liberalism.[2]

While the meanings of liberalism and democracy are historically and conceptually fraught, the contemporary discourse of liberal democratic crisis assumes a few minimal definitions. Within this discourse, liberalism means something like "the protection of the rights of minorities and individuals, guarantees of citizens' liberty, and the subjection of the government to the constraints imposed by the rule of law."[3] And democracy means something like "the combination of popular sovereignty and majority rule."[4] Given the size of the population of nearly all modern nation-states, that combination is thought to require a representative mechanism: comparatively free, fair, and competitive elections, in which the people choose representatives to govern their common life.

It is not the goal of this essay to quibble with the above definitions, or to call into question the utility of heuristic frameworks such as illiberal democracy versus undemocratic liberalism and populism versus technocracy. I assume that both the definitions and the frameworks reference—however imprecisely—a real world of institutions, ideas, and social movements that exist—however complexly—beyond the confines of scholarly debate.

The goal of the essay is rather to ask where administration or administrative government fits within the contemporary discourse of liberal democratic crisis. If two constitutive features of liberal democratic nation-states are liberalism and democracy, administration is a third feature that has been integral to those states' development and persistence over time, as well as to their present predicament.

What is administration, or administrative government? It is government not by legislatures, courts, or elected members of the executive branch (such as presidents and prime ministers), but by administrators who are subject to the supervision of all the other branches of government, while not being fully identified with any of them. Whether selected by meritocratic procedures or appointed by elected officials, these administrators work within "agencies" or "departments" or "commissions." There, their task is to implement in detail the broad national policies approved by the people's elected representatives in the legislative and executive branches.

History demonstrates that where liberal democratic nation-states have emerged from the shocks of industrialization and globalization, so too has administrative government.[5] This fact is not surprising given that to govern any sufficiently large, populous territory—particularly under conditions of industrialization and globalization—is to govern administratively. The very generality of this point, however, has given rise to considerable anxiety within liberal democratic nation-states, as administrative government is every bit as much a feature of illiberal and undemocratic regimes as liberal and democratic ones. Throughout the first two-thirds of the twentieth century, the effort to distinguish the administrative governments of liberal-democratic nation-states from those of their fascist and communist rivals was a major preoccupation of American and European lawyers and politicians.[6]

Where does the ineluctability of administrative government fit within the contemporary discourse of liberal democratic crisis? At first, this question would seem to have an easy answer: rule by administration—rule by electorally unaccountable bureaucrats—is technocracy, or undemocratic liberalism. The answer is not so simple for at least two reasons. First, because many of the staunchest defenders of administrative government in the liberal democratic world view administration as a vital organ of *democracy* itself.[7] If administrative government is vital to democratic legitimacy, to channeling and achieving the ends of the people themselves, then to align administration on the side of undemocratic liberalism is nonsensical. The second reason why a simple conflation of administrative government with technocracy, or undemocratic liberalism, is unworkable is that many of the staunchest critics of administrative government in the liberal democratic world see it as a mortal threat to *liberalism*—to individual and minority rights, to the liberty of citizens, and to the rule of law.[8]

Administrative government, then, seems to be both too democratic and too illiberal to perform the functions of undemocratic liberalism. Perhaps administrative government is then more sensibly identified with illiberal democracy, or populism? Hardly. Populists in general disdain administrative decision-making as a technocratic domination of the public sphere, terminally undemocratic yet also often too liberal in its circumscription of valid administrative ends.[9]

Given that administrative government satisfies neither technocrats nor populists, one might be tempted to argue instead that such government is most at home within the liberal-democratic nation-state itself. From this perspective, the persistence of administration would be a sign of liberal democratic stability, rather than liberal democratic crisis. And yet, as discussed above, all industrial and post-industrial nation-states, not just liberal-democratic ones, have featured administrative government. Just as importantly, all industrial and post-industrial liberal-democratic nation-states have experienced recurrent crises concerning the threat that administrative government poses to liberal and democratic governance.[10] Administrative government lives everywhere but is never truly at home. Within liberal democratic nation states in particular, administrative government appears as both a vital organ and a potentially malignant mass of cells.

Current debates among scholars and practitioners of American administrative law exemplify the puzzling role that administrative government plays within the broader discourse of liberal democratic crisis.[11] Previously confined to seminar rooms, law reviews, and the occasional federal court, these debates about the legitimacy of administrative government have achieved a new prominence thanks to the political polarization of the executive and legislative branches during the Obama presidency, the rise to power of Donald Trump and his early, anti-administrative supporters, such as Steve Bannon, and twenty years of unprecedented Republican success in appointing judges skeptical of administrative government to the federal courts.

Some might find it surprising that scholars and practitioners of administrative law spend any time at all debating the legitimacy of administration. If administration exists, and there are laws that govern its functioning, then practitioners and scholars of that law presumably have their hands full. To understand why debates about administrative legitimacy nonetheless persist within the precincts of administrative law, it helps to say a few words about the historical function of administrative law, as distinct from the historical function of public administration as such.

Administrative law, at least as it has developed since the late nineteenth century in the Anglo-American world, purports to submit administration—understood to be tendentially illiberal and tendentially undemocratic—to liberal and democratic norms. Center-left or "progressive" defenders of the American administrative state claim that it still performs this function, and admirably. They emphasize the forms of supervision and control to which federal administrators are subject by the executive, legislative, and judicial branches of government, as well as the forms of "internal administrative law" that administrators themselves produce, internal processes that preserve individual rights and other rule-of-law values.[12] Right-leaning critics claim that administrative law no longer works to check the illiberal and undemocratic tendencies of the administrative state and call for the restoration of a prior, more liberal, and democratic order.[13] Some heterodox theorists—Adrian Vermeule in particular—take a different tack, arguing that administrative law has largely worked to develop and legitimate necessarily illiberal modes of government that liberalism and democracy themselves turned out to require.[14]

In a striking passage at the opening of his recent book *Law's Abnegation*, Vermeule writes:

> Although in earlier eras law claimed (rightly or not) to represent the overarching impartial power that resolved and reconciled local conflicts over the activities of government, the long arc of the law has bent steadily toward deference—a freely chosen deference to the administrative state. Law has abnegated its authority, relegating itself to the margins of governmental arrangements. Although there is still a sense in which law is constitutive of the administrative state, that is so only in a thin sense—the way a picture frame can be constitutive of the picture yet otherwise unimportant, compared to the rich content at the center.[15]

While Vermeule celebrates the abnegation of law, many on both the left and right see in the developments that Vermeule describes the dread spread of illiberalism through the formerly liberal democratic nation-states of the transatlantic world. In his avocational writings on public affairs, Vermeule has not sought to assuage anxious liberals.[16] Rather, he hails the promise of administratively driven social reforms, reforms that are denounced as illiberal by prominent legal commentators in the United States, Europe, and elsewhere. However heterodox, Vermeule's open celebration of the administrative achievement of controversial social goods represents the true challenge of illiberalism that progressive administrative law scholars are at pains to overcome.

This challenge is made all the more difficult by the fact that progressives also reject the traditional checks on the illiberal tendencies of administrative government: more invasive judicial review of administrative decision-making; and the imposition of more painstaking decision-making procedures that replicate the adversarial, deliberative, and transparent qualities of decision-making in the courtroom and the legislative chamber.[17] These checks—which taken together could be called, somewhat tendentiously, the legalization of the administrative process—is the one preferred by conservative critics of American administrative government.[18]

The progressive response to both the conservatives and the Vermeullians is that American administrative government is plenty lawlike already. Contra Vermeule, no abnegation has occurred, and therefore, contra the conservatives, no new rounds of legalistic reform are necessary. If anything, progressives continue to insist that administrative government suffers from too many legalistic fetters, and they argue that more of these fetters could be removed without any risk to the liberalism of the administrative process.[19]

The progressive response is unavailing, for at least two interrelated reasons. First, the internal administrative law that progressives hail as a substitute for quasi-judicial and quasi-legislative procedures may well be adequate from the perspective of justice (or scientific rationality, or other commendable values), but it is not adequate from the perspective of *liberalism*, commonly understood.[20] Second, the parallel attempt by progressives to demonstrate that administrative government is adequately democratic undermines their account of the adequacy of its liberalism. This is because the democratic features of administration (such as presidential and legislative supervision, and public participation) regularly put pressure on administration's more liberal features (such as regularity, neutrality, rights protection, etc.).[21] This dynamic leads to continual efforts by administrative apologists to explain how democratic inputs do not, in fact, violate administrative government's more lawlike features. These efforts are frustrated by the fact that democracy and liberalism exist in considerable tension with one another. If administrative government works at all, it works by exacerbating this tension, not by resolving it.

To see how, it is useful to introduce three relatively technical questions that structure the current debate between progressive defenders and conservative critics of American administrative government.

First, to what extent should Congress be able to delegate to administrative government the task of shaping federal law, rather than shaping such law itself through the normal (and exceedingly cumbersome) legislative process? Since the New Deal, courts have proven exceedingly reluctant to second-guess Congress's decision to delegate law-making power to administrators. Progressives are more than happy to preserve this status quo, while some conservative judges, politicians, and scholars have called for its revision. One such revision would require that every administrative rule that significantly impacts the economy be approved by majorities of both the House and Senate before going into effect.[22]

Second, what degree of deference should judges extend to administrative decision-makers? Common answers range from declining to review administrative decisions at all to making an independent judgment about the quality of the evidence, procedures, and legal reasoning on which administrative decision makers relied.

Third, what degree of procedural protection should private parties receive when they are regulated by a given administrative agency? The answer here is always multifaceted, but conservative critics tend to prefer procedures that either (1) resemble those used in a court of law, when administrators apply preexisting rules to the past conduct of individual parties; or (2) that allow for extensive, public deliberation and multiple rounds of testimony from interested parties, when administrators craft general rules that will apply prospectively to all similarly situated parties. Progressives, on the other hand, contend that such quasi-judicial and quasi-legislative procedures are often too cumbersome, too skeptical of administrative expertise, and too prone to manipulation by wealthy corporations and lobbyists.

In giving their own answers to the three foregoing questions (concerning the proper extent of congressional delegation, judicial supervision, and procedural protection), progressive scholars have developed a theory of administrative government that emphasizes its peculiar mix of democratic and liberal bona fides. This theory begins with a highly plausible historical and pragmatic answer to the first question: the delegation of power to make legally binding decisions from Congress to administrative agencies is a centuries-old practice that also happens to be unavoidable in a populous, industrial, or post-industrial nation-state.[23] Having assumed this much, progressive theorists then endeavor to show why administrative government can be trusted to wield its delegated power in a reliably democratic and liberal manner. According to progressive theory, the primary democratic check on administrative government is presidential supervision, supplemented from below by bouts of public participation in administrative decision-making.[24]

The primary liberal check, meanwhile, is internal administrative law—a body of administratively generated rules, customs, and practices that structure how administrators behave, and render that behavior more rather than less consistent, fair, and protective of individual rights.[25] Some of these rules, customs, and practices are intentionally created and relatively formal. Others are emergent felicities. All are the product of cooperation and competition between administrators within a given agency, administrators across agencies, and administrators and the White House. In one recent, synoptic account, Gillian Metzger and Kevin Stack define internal administrative law as the law, or lawlike system, produced by all the "policies, procedures, practices, [and] oversight mechanisms" that are "internal" to the executive branch, rather than imposed upon it by Congress and, especially, the courts.[26] So defined, internal administrative law has always existed. Yet, as Metzger and Stack go on to argue, the phenomenon appears to be of growing importance to both practitioners and scholars of administrative government:

> More and more, presidents and executive branch officials rely on internal issuances and internal administration to achieve policy goals and govern effectively. . . . To give just a few examples: interagency arrangements are important parts of recent environmental and financial regulation and national security initiatives; guidance and enforcement policy play an increasingly central role in education and employment contexts; and administrative oversight, negotiated agreements, and funding protocols have significantly affected the shape of contemporary federalism. Equally, if not more, significant is the growing number of issuances from centralized entities like the Office of Management and Budget (OMB) and its Office of Information and Regulatory Affairs (OIRA), governing everything from regulatory promulgation and analysis to agency use of guidance, budgeting, enforcement policy, and peer review.
>
> Administrative law scholarship has also gone internal. Agency design and coordination, centralized White House control, the civil service and internal separation of powers, internal supervision, the role of agency guidance—these are just some of the topics now receiving sustained scholarly analysis.[27]

What explains this growth in the volume and significance of internal administrative law? Most scholars who have studied the phenomenon point to a mix of political, regulatory, and jurisprudential developments. At the political level, Metzger and Stack are not alone in emphasizing "political polarization and partisan gridlock" within the legislature.[28] At the regulatory level, a set of interrelated changes to the form and focus of administrative government have each tended to spur agencies' production of internal administrative law: growth in the perceived complexity and uncertainty of commercial, environmental, and technological problems; a shift away from command-and-control-style regulation and toward greater cooperation between federal agencies, private corporations, and state governments; and, finally, a tendency to "securitize" various regulatory challenges, that is, to treat those challenges from the point of view of emergency management and national security.[29] Finally, at the jurisprudential level, internal administrative law can be understood as a strategic response to the federal courts' increasing willingness to second-guess more tractable kinds of administrative decision-making, such as procedurally intensive administrative rule making and administrative adjudication. The result of this strategic play—less formal, less transparent, and less legally legible forms of administrative law-making—was certainly not intended by already-skeptical judges, and it does not satisfy their doubts about the lawfulness of the administrative process. But internal administrative law does make administrative decision-making somewhat more difficult to attack directly in the courts.

These explanations for the growth of internal administrative law could, of course, be used to question its liberal pedigree. Why should administrators seeking to work around partisan gridlock, to exert mastery over complex social and natural problems, or to mitigate judicial interference, be trusted to regulate themselves in a manner consistent with the regularity, neutrality, and respect for individual rights that one associates with liberal governance? One answer to this question occasionally suggested by progressives is that democratic checks—such as presidential control and public participation—can help to push back against illiberal deformations of internal administrative law. But this answer makes sense only if we assume that the politicians and publics who influence the administrative state themselves favor liberal outcomes. That is not an assumption that progressives are willing to make consistently over time and across fields of regulation.[30] A different sociological assumption has proven more appealing to progressives seeking to establish internal administrative law's liberal bona fides. This assumption is that the same professional discipline and technical expertise that enable administrators to forge the rules, customs, and practices of internal administrative law also imbue that law with a reliably liberal cast. Whether a given administrator's expertise lies in the natural sciences, the social sciences, medicine, or law, the social experience of professionalization itself, as well as the overarching commitment to lawful action in the public interest that inclines administrators of every stripe to be particularly deferential to the legal experts within their ranks, helps to ensure that internal administrative law satisfies norms of regularity, neutrality, and respect for individual rights.[31] Undergirded by this sociological assumption of a particular kind of professional—and therefore liberal—administrative class, the concept of internal administrative law is crucial to rebutting both conservative critics of administrative government (who claim that administration as it currently exists in the United States traduces the rule of law) and administrative government's heterodox defenders (who affirm and applaud its illiberalism).

The resulting picture of an administrative state in democratic and liberal equilibrium, shored up by presidentialism and public participation on the one hand, and professionalism and internal administrative law on the other, provides reliably progressive answers to the second two questions raised above. Those questions concern the optimal degree of judicial review of administrative decision-making, and the optimal degree of procedural constraint that Congress and the courts should impose on administrative decision-making. The answers favor judicial refusal to review a range of administrative decisions relating to resource allocation and enforcement policy; judicial deference to administrative fact-finding and administrators' interpretations of the statutes that they are tasked with implementing; and judicial and legislative restraint when it comes to imposing decision-making procedures more onerous than those that administrators themselves have determined are most efficient and fair.

But it is reasonable to reject the progressive picture of an administrative state in democratic and liberal equilibrium, and thus also to be skeptical of progressive answers to more technical questions concerning the administrative state's relationship to Congress, the judiciary, and the people whom it regulates. There are two fundamental problems with the progressive picture. The first is that the putative sources of democratic and liberal legitimation of administrative decision-making—presidentialism, public participation, professionalism, and internal administrative law—are unreliably democratic and unreliably liberal. The second is that these sources, to the extent that each does provide some modicum of democratic or liberal legitimation, undermine one another.

There already exist important and troubling critiques of the democratic bona fides of presidentialism and public participation.[32] I will not rehearse them at length. The fundamental point of these critiques is that neither presidential pressure nor pressure from those private parties subject to a given regulatory scheme satisfy our intuitive sense of what it would mean for a national polity to govern itself, however representatively. While such pressures can and do influence administrative decision-making, they cannot supply the quality of deliberation or represent the diversity of interests that a functioning legislature would. That being said, the United States does not have a functioning legislature. In light of this fact, the democratic argument for administrative government is the strongest one available to progressives (as well as to other, more heterodox defenders of administration, such as Adrian Vermeule and his sometimes co-author, Eric Posner).

The progressive defense is weakest at two other points: its claim that professionalism and internal administrative law provide an adequate substitute for more traditional judicial and legislative means of protecting liberal values such as regularity, neutrality, and respect for individual rights; and its assumption that the putatively democratic sources of administrative legitimation—presidentialism and public participation—do not undermine whatever liberal legitimation might be supplied by professionalism and internal administrative law.

Administrative law's flight from judicial control is a perilous road for progressives to travel. The striking symmetry—at times identity—between progressive defenses of the administrative state and those offered by openly illiberal theorists calls not so much for pause as for reorientation. How did progressives get themselves into this mess, and where are they trying to go? Viewing the courts as the chief obstacle to progressive governance is an old theme, and contemporary progressives trace their preferred countermeasures to a well-pedigreed source: the New Deal.[33] But what they miss in resuscitating New Deal–era arguments for presidentialism and professionalism is that these arguments depended on a sociological analysis of the courts as the representatives not of a particular party but of a particular class.[34] From this perspective, presidential and professional control of the administrative state was a second-best or third-best solution, one that would only be successful in advancing progressive reforms to the extent that the president and the professionals could be sufficiently autonomous from the class fractions that the judiciary represented—the large capitalists and the upper echelons of corporate management.

New Deal reformers were quite explicit about the potential for, and the desirability of, class differentiation across the federal government. Their optimism can be attributed in large part to certain contingencies of the period, relating to the social composition of the federal bureaucracy and the Democratic Party. New Deal agencies were largely staffed by an aspiring middle class with close ties to urban immigrant communities and rural backwaters. While some administrators, particularly some of the lawyers, enjoyed elite educations, many did not, and most came to Washington in part because they were excluded, for socioeconomic reasons, from the traditional pathways of elite professional development in the private sector.[35] As such, the New Deal's administrative class reflected the increasingly multiethnic and working-class base of the New Deal–era Democratic Party. This party's base, in turn, exerted a disciplining effect on its political representatives, the president in particular.

The role of the Democratic Party's social base in shaping New Deal racial policy—often for the worse, given the power of white Southerners within the Democratic coalition—has recently received great attention.[36] But the influence of large, economically marginalized social blocs also helped to insulate New Deal governance from corporate capture. So too did divisions within the corporate sector itself, as the leading labor-intensive and capital-intensive firms vied against one another for control over industrial and trade policy.[37] Whether the resulting New Deal state was conducive to liberal democracy remains a fair question. But its departures from liberal democratic norms could be understood, and defended, as the price to be paid for establishing countervailing socioeconomic power within the executive branch.

Today the situation is quite different. Rising inequality, declining social mobility, and the consolidation of an alliance between the most productive and powerful firms, an increasingly self-reproducing professional class, and the Democratic Party itself—all these trends make it difficult for contemporary progressives to offer a hopeful compromise between liberalism, democracy, and countervailing economic power.[38] Today, there is less room than ever between the social composition of the judiciary and the upper echelons of the administrative state, and less connection than ever between the upper echelons of the administrative state and the median private-sector worker. Nor has the contemporary Democratic Party's social base proven capable of imposing working-class priorities on the administrative state in times of Democratic control. Given these dynamics, an administrative state whose legality rests on external presidential control and internal professional control risks sacrificing liberal ideals for no greater cause than the entrenchment of the prerogatives of those firms and professionals associated with high-productivity sectors of the economy. Perhaps that entrenchment is far preferable to the social chaos on offer from the party of Trump and the courts under its sway. But under present conditions, the progressive vision of administrative legality departs not only from liberal ideals, but also from the sort of economic democracy imagined by New Deal reformers.

While many aspects of this story are distinctly American, the peculiar status of administrative government, as both a deviation from liberal democracy and a frustration to illiberal democrats and undemocratic liberals, has become a global phenomenon. Over the course of the twentieth century, the struggle to maintain, defend, and spread liberal democratic capitalism required the construction of ever more powerful administrative states. Administrative government thus became liberal democracy's eerie double, a necessary supplement that also functions like a funhouse mirror: reflecting and attempting to resolve the fundamental tension between liberalism and democracy even as it distorts the meaning of those concepts.

At the dawn of the twenty-first century, a group of French sociologists explained this mirror-like relationship between administrative government and liberal democracy in terms of a fateful "double delegation": the delegation from citizens to political representatives, and from laypersons to technical experts.[39] Each delegation alienates from members of mass society their capacity to learn, to deliberate, and to decide. The combination and iteration of the two delegations constitute what is now recognizable as administrative government. In administrative government, political representatives act as a proxy for democratic decision-making, and technical experts act as a proxy for liberal decision-making. While direct public participation in the administrative process, and the development by experts of self-binding rules, customs, and practices, can enrich the thin forms of democracy and liberalism that survive the double delegation, they do not alter the fundamental alienation of power from citizens and laypersons that administrative government entails. Nor do they resolve the persistent tension between even the thinnest forms of democracy and liberalism, as conflicts between political and technical delegates continually call into question the legitimacy, rationality, and fairness of administrative decision-making.

In this context, illiberal democracy and undemocratic liberalism are most usefully understood as expressions of the desire to overcome the alienations that constitute administrative government, and to resolve the internal conflicts among political representatives and technical experts that come to preoccupy it. Meanwhile, actually existing liberal democratic societies are so dependent on administrative government that they cannot help but become identified with it, their ideals compromised by it. The crisis of liberal democracy, then, is a function of liberal democratic success. For populous, capitalist nation-states, the condition of that success was the adoption of administrative government. While administrative government need be neither fully illiberal nor fully antidemocratic, its very effort to embody liberal and democratic values tends to distort those values, and to accentuate their contradictions. To the extent that defenders of administrative government ask us to accept unconvincing and ineffective proxies for liberalism and democracy as the things themselves, they feed the desire for less alienating and contradictory—if often more unjust—alternatives.

Notes

1. For a useful overview, see Shari Berman, "The Pipe Dream of Undemocratic Liberalism," *Journal of Democracy* 28 (July 2017): 29. The term "illiberal democracy" is generally attributed to Fareed Zakaria, "The Rise of Illiberal Democracy," *Foreign Affairs* 76 (November–December 1997): 22. For other recent discussions, see Nadia Urbinati, *Me the People: How Populism Transforms Democracy* (Cambridge, MA: Harvard University Press, 2019); Yascha Mounk, *The People v. Democracy* (Cambridge, MA: Harvard University Press, 2018); Cas Mudde and Cristóbal Rovira Kaltwasser, eds., *Populism in Europe and the Americas: Threat or Corrective for Democracy?* (Cambridge: Cambridge University Press, 2012); Christopher Bickerton and Carlo Invernizzi Accetti, "Populism and Technocracy: Opposites or Complements?," *Critical Review of International Social and Political Philosophy* 20 (2017): 186; Jan-Werner Mueller, "Protecting Popular Self-Government from the People," *Annual Review of Political Science* 19 (2016): 249; Elliott Norton, "Illiberal Democrats versus Undemocratic Liberals: The Struggle over the Future of Thailand's Fragile Democracy," *Asian Journal of Political Science* 20 (April 2012): 46; and Camilla Vergara, "Systemic Corruption: Constitutional Ideas for an Anti-Oligarchic Republic" (Ph.D. diss., Columbia University, 2019). Note that Berman's association of technocracy with undemocratic *liberalism* is itself contingent, bound up with the political and legal culture of the contemporary capitalist West. It is logically possible to imagine, and historically easy to identify, illiberal technocracies.

2. See, e.g., Berman, "The Pipe Dream of Undemocratic Liberalism," 37. ("Technocracy and populism are evil political twins, each feeding off and intensifying the other. The first seeks to limit democracy to save liberalism, while the second seeks to limit liberalism to save democracy.") Berman notes correctly that populism has traditionally set itself against oligarchy, rule by the elite or the few, rather than technocracy. In contemporary liberal democracies, however, oligarchy has few *explicit* defenders. It is rule by experts—judges, central bankers, public health officials, and other professional decision makers who are assumed to be apolitical—that is offered as a legitimate alternative to rule by the masses. Populists, in turn, have tended to direct their ire at technocratic means of solving social problems. See generally Bickerton and Invernizzi Accetto, "Populism and Technocracy," 8–10.

3. Norton, "Illiberal Democrats versus Undemocratic Liberals," 64.

4. Cas Mudde and Cristóbal Rovira Kaltwasser, "Populism and (Liberal) Democracy: A Framework for Analysis," in Mudde and Kaltwasser, *Populism in Europe and the Americas*, 1, 10.

5. See generally Susan Rose-Ackerman, ed., *Comparative Administrative Law* (Northampton, MA: Edwin Elgar, 2010). For the even deeper roots of administrative government, see, e.g., Jerry Mashaw, *Creating the Administrative Constitution* (New Haven, CT: Yale University Press, 2012).

6. For a brief historical overview, see Jeremy K. Kessler, "A War for Liberty: On the Law of Conscientious Objection," in *The Cambridge History of the Second World War*, vol. 3, ed. Michael Geyer and Adam Tooze (Cambridge: Cambridge University Press, 2015), 447.

7. See, e.g., Peter L. Lindseth, *Power and Legitimacy* (Oxford: Oxford University Press, 2010); Jerry Mashaw, *Reasoned Administration and Democratic Legitimacy* (Cambridge: Cambridge University Press, 2018); Pierre Rosanvallon, *Democratic Legitimacy* (Princeton, NJ: Princeton University Press, 2008); William Scheuerman, *Liberal Democracy and the Social Acceleration of Time* (Baltimore: Johns Hopkins University Press, 2004); Samuel Moyn, "On Human Rights and Majority Politics: Felix Frankfurter's Democratic Theory," *Vanderbilt Journal of Transnational Law* 52 (2019): 1135; Eric Posner and Adrian Vermeule, "Tyrannophobia," in *Comparative Constitutional Design*, ed. Tom Ginsburg (2012), 317.

8. See, e.g., Bruce Ackerman, *The Decline and Fall of the American Republic* (Cambridge, MA: Harvard University Press, 2010); Philip Hamburger, *Is Administrative Law Unlawful?* (Chicago: University of Chicago Press, 2016); Matthias Ruffert, ed., *The Transformation of Administrative Law in Europe* (Oxford: Oxford University Press, 2007); Roberto Mangabeira Unger, *The Critical Legal Studies Movement: Another Time, A Greater Task* (London: Verso Books, 2015); Paul Dragos Alicia, "Public Administration and the Classical Liberal Perspective: Criticism, Clarifications, and Reconstruction," *Administration & Society* 49 (2017): 530; Michael C. Behrent, "Foucault and France's Liberal Moment," in *In Search of the Liberal Moment* (London: Palgrave Macmillan, 2016), ed. Stephen W. Sawyer and Iain Stewart, 155, 162–164; Steven G. Calabresi and Gary Lawson, "The Depravity of the 1930s and the Modern Administrative State," *Notre Dame Law Review* 94 (2018): 821 (2018); and Gwendal Châton, "Taking Anti-totalitarianism Seriously: The Emergence of the Aronian Circle in the 1970s," in Sawyer and Stewart, *In Search of the Liberal Moment*, 17.

9. See generally Margaret Canovan, *Populism* (Toronto: Junction Books,1981); Ernesto Laclau, *On Populist Reason* (London: Verso Books, 2005); Vergara, "Systemic Corruption."

10. See, e.g., James O. Freedman, *Crisis and Legitimacy* (Cambridge: Cambridge University Press, 1978); William Scheuerman, *Between the Norm and the Exception: The Frankfurt School and the Rule of Law* (Cambridge, MA: MIT Press, 1994); Peter L. Lindseth, "Reconciling with the Past: John Willis and the Question of Judicial Review in Inter-War and Post-War England," *University of Toronto Law Journal* 55 (2005): 657; Peter L. Lindseth, "The Paradox of Parliamentary Supremacy: Delegation, Democracy, and Dictatorship in Germany and France, 1920s–1950s," *Yale Law Journal* 113 (2004): 1341; and Michael Taggart, "From 'Parliamentary Powers' to Privatization: The Chequered History of Delegated Legislation in the Twentieth Century," *University of Toronto Law Journal* 55 (2005): 575.

11. See generally Jeremy K. Kessler, "The Struggle for Administrative Legitimacy," *Harvard Law Review* 29 (2016): 718; Gillian Metzger, "Foreword: 1930s Redux: The Administrative State Under Siege," *Harvard Law Review* 131 (2017): 1.

12. See, e.g., Daniel Ernst, *Tocqueville's Nightmare: The Administrative Emerges in America* (Oxford: Oxford University Press, 2014); Mashaw, *Creating the Administrative Constitution*; Nicholas Parrillo, ed., *Administrative Law from the Inside Out* (Cambridge: Cambridge University Press, 2017); Daniel A. Farber and Anne Joseph O'Connell, "Agencies as Adversaries," *California. Law Review* 105 (2017); Abbe Gluck, Anne Joseph O'Connell, and Rosa Po, "Unorthodox Lawmaking, Unorthodox Rulemaking," *Columbia Law Review* 115 (2015): 1789; Neal Kumar Katyal, "Internal Separation of Powers: Checking Today's Most Dangerous Branch from Within," *Yale Law Journal* 115 (2006): 2314; Elizabeth Magill and Adrian Vermeule, "Allocating Power within Agencies," *Yale Law Journal* 120 (2011): 1032; Metzger, "1930s Redux"; Gillian E. Metzger and Kevin M. Stack, "Internal Administrative Law," *Michigan Law Review* 115 (2017): 1239; Jon D. Michaels, "Of Constitutional Custodians and Regulatory Rivals: An Account of the Old and New Separation of Powers," *New York University Law* 91 (2016): 227; Trevor W. Morrison, "Constitutional Alarmism," *Harvard Law Review* 124 (2011): 1688; Noah Rosenblum, "The Antifascist Roots of Presidential Administration," *Columbia Law Review* 122 (2022); Edward P. Rubin, "The Myth of Accountability and the Anti-Administrative Impulse," *Michigan Law Review* 103 (2005): 2073; Cass Sunstein and Adrian Vermeule, "Libertarian Administrative Law," *University of Chicago Law Review* 82 (2015): 393.

13. See, e.g., Hamburger, *Is Administrative Law Unlawful?*; Lawson and Calabresi, "The Depravity of the 1930s and the Modern Administrative State."

14. See, e.g., Eric Posner and Adrian Vermeule, *The Executive Unbound: After the Madisonian Republic* (Oxford: Oxford University Press, 2010); Adrian Vermeule, *Law's Abnegation: From Law's Empire to the Administrative State* (Cambridge, MA: Harvard University Press, 2016).

15. Vermeule, *Law's Abnegation*, 1.

16. See, e.g., Adrian Vermeule, "Integration from Within," *American Affairs* 2 (Spring 2018), https://americanaffairsjournal.org/2018/02/integration-from-within/.

17. See generally Ernst, *Tocqueville's Nightmare*; Joanna Grisinger, *The Unwieldy American State: Administrative Politics since the New Deal* (Cambridge: Cambridge University Press, 2012); Jeremy K. Kessler, "New Look Constitutionalism," *University of Pennsylvania Law Review* 167 (2019): 1749.

18. See, e.g., Calabresi and Lawson, "The Depravity of the 1930s and the Modern Administrative State."

19. See, e.g., Nicholas Bagley, "The Procedure Fetish," *Michigan Law Review* 118 (2019): 345.

20. Self-regulation by a mix of political appointees and career civil servants within administrative agencies is not the same as review of those agencies by an independent judiciary; such self-regulation does not serve the same values, or produce the same outcomes, as judicial review. Nor does internal self-regulation, however leavened with public participation by interested private parties, serve the same values and produce the same outcomes as the passage of general and prospective rules by majority vote of a body of elected representatives. Administrative self-regulation is a different mode of governance than the liberal mode of governance. See, e.g., Anders Esmark, "Limits to Liberal Government: An Alternative History of Governmentality," *Administration & Society* 50 (2018): 240; Cynthia R. Farina, "The Consent of the Governed: Against Simple Rules for a Complex World," *Chicago-Kent Law Review* 72 (1997): 987.

21. For an illuminating discussion of the problem in the context of presidential supervision, see Daphna Renan, "The President's Two Bodies," *Columbia Law Review* 120 (2020): 1178–84. See also Daphna Renan, "Presidential Norms and Article II," *Harvard Law Review* 131 (2018), 2278. ("[L]inking the legitimacy of the administrative state to democratic accountability through the President, in turn, reinforced norms of presidential control over agency policymaking. And those norms over time contributed to a less stable and more ideologically polarized policymaking apparatus inside the executive branch.")

22. Compare Metzger, "1930s Redux," 87–90, with Calabresi and Lawson, "The Depravity of the 1930s and the Modern Administrative State," 855–56.

23. See generally Mashaw, *Creating the Administrative Constitution*; Maggie Blackhawk, "Petitioning and the Making of the Administrative State," *Yale Law Journal* 127 (2018): 1538; Gillian E. Metzger, "The Constitutional Duty to Supervise," *Yale Law Journal* 124 (2015): 1837; Nicholas R. Parrillo, "A Critical Assessment of the Originalist Case against Administrative Regulatory Power: New Evidence from the Federal Tax on Private Real Estate in the 1790s," *Yale Law Journal* 130 (2021): 1288; Keith E. Whittington and Jason Iuliano, "The Myth of the Nondelegation Doctrine," *University of Pennsylvania Law Review* 165 (2017): 379.

24. For the classic statement, see Elena Kagan, "Presidential Administration," *Harvard Law Review* 114 (2001): 2245.

25. For the classic statement, see Jerry L. Mashaw, *Bureaucratic Justice: Managing Social Security Disability Claims* (New Haven, CT: Yale University Press, 1983). For a contemporary account, see Metzger and Stack, "Internal Administrative Law." Concepts related to, and often by encompassed by, internal administrative law are "internal checks and balances" and "internal separation of powers."

26. Metzger and Stack, "Internal Administrative Law," 1244.

27. Metzger and Stack, 1241–43.

28. Metzger and Stack, 1242.

29. See, e.g., Metzger, "The Constitutional Duty to Supervise," 1849–58.

30. Indeed, if the assumption was generalizable, there would be far less need for internal administrative law as a liberalizing force within the administrative state.

31. A similar argument was made by future Supreme Court Justice Felix Frankfurter in his seminal article "The Task of Administrative Law," *University of Pennsylvania Law Review* 75 (1927): 614. For further discussion of the relationship between professionalism and internal administrative law, see Jeremy K. Kessler and Charles Sabel, "The Uncertain Future of Administrative Law," *Daedalus* (2021): 188–207. For more on the influence of lawyers on both liberalism and administration, see Robert W. Gordon, "Legal Thought and Legal Practice in the Age of American Enterprise, 1870–1920," in *Professions and Professional Ideologies in America*, ed. Gerald L. Geison (Chapel Hill: University of North Carolina Press, 1983), 95; and Terrence C. Halliday and Lucien Karpik, "Politics Matter: A Comparative Theory of Lawyers in the Making of Political Liberalism," in *Lawyers and the Rise of Western Political Liberalism* (Oxford: Clarendon Press, 1997), 20–34.

32. See, e.g., Peter M. Shane, *Madison's Nightmare: How Executive Power Threatens American Democracy* (Chicago: University of Chicago Press, 2009); Farina, "The Consent of the Governed"; Samuel Issacharoff, "Democracy's Deficits," *University of Chicago Law Review* 85 (2018): 485; Jerry L. Mashaw and David Berke, "Presidential Administration in a Regime of Separated Powers: An Analysis of Recent American Experience," *Yale Journal of Regulation* 35 (2018): 549; Jide Nzelibe, "The Fable of the Nationalist President and the Parochial Congress," *UCLA Law Review* 3 (2006): 1217; Wendy E. Wagner, "Administrative Law, Filter Failure, and Information Capture," *Duke Law Journal* 59 (2010): 1321; Note, "Civic Republican Administrative Theory: Bureaucrats as Deliberative Democrats," *Harvard Law Review* 103 (1994): 1401.

33. See, e.g., Metzger, "1930s Redux"; Rosenblum, "Antifascist Roots of Presidential Administration."

34. See generally Robert H. Jackson, *The Struggle against Judicial Supremacy: A Study of Crisis in American Power Politics* (New York: Knopf, 1941); Edward A. Purcell Jr., *Brandeis and the Progressive Constitution* (New Haven, CT: Yale University Press, 2000). For further discussion, see Kessler, "The Struggle for Administrative Legitimacy."

35. See generally Peter H. Irons, *The New Deal Lawyers* (Princeton, NJ: Princeton University Press, 1982); Ronen Shamir, *Managing Legal Uncertainty: Elite Lawyers in the New Deal* (Durham, NC: Duke University Press, 1992).

36. See, e.g., Ira Katznelson, *Fear Itself: The New Deal and the Origins of Our Time* (New York: Norton, 2013).

37. See Thomas Ferguson, *Golden Rule: The Investment Theory of Party Competition and the Logic of Money-Driven Political Systems* (Chicago: University of Chicago Press, 1995), 113–240.

38. See, e.g., Catherine Liu, *Virtue Hoarders* (Minneapolis: University of Minnesota Press, 2021); Michael Lind, *The New Class War* (New York: Penguin Random House, 2020); Daniel Markovits, *The Meritocracy Trap* (New York: Penguin Random House, 2019).

39. Michel Callon, Pierre Lascoumes, and Yannick Barthe, *Acting in an Uncertain World: An Essay on Technical Democracy* (Cambridge, MA: MIT Press, 2009). While delegation is an age-old tool of governance, the combination of political and technical delegation along with its normalization as the preferred solution to every social problem are distinctive to industrial and post-industrial liberal and state capitalist societies.

CHAPTER 4

Post-Truth as a Precursor to Authoritarianism

Lee McIntyre

> It is the essence of power that it accrues to those with the ability to determine the nature of the real.
>
> —Christopher Bigsby, introduction to *The Crucible*

What Is Post-Truth?

The phenomenon of "post-truth" has been defined by the Oxford Dictionaries as "relating to or denoting circumstances in which objective facts are less influential in shaping public opinion than appeals to emotion and personal belief."[1] As such, it is part of—or perhaps the culmination of—a campaign of fact and truth denial that has been going on in Western democracies for the last several decades. On scientific topics such as evolution, climate change, and whether vaccines cause autism, the forces of ideology, cognitive bias, media confusion, and financial interest have conspired to spread disinformation and legitimize doubt about even the most settled factual questions. Where there is room for genuine scientific skepticism, this has been pounced on by cherry-pickers and conspiracy theorists who hope to use any ambiguity or uncertainty not toward the desired end of corroborating the scientific attitude of testing and openness, but rather as a means to endorse a conclusion that they have already decided must be true. Even where there is no room for legitimate doubt, sometimes it is created anyway.

In the 2016 US presidential election—and in the earlier Brexit vote in the United Kingdom—we saw this attitude metastasize into an all-out assault on facts, truth, reality, and evidence of any kind, when it did not fit the reality desired by various political interests. In Britain, a bogus statistic was plastered on the sides of buses everywhere, which convinced many that the UK was sending 350 million GBP a week to the EU, when nothing like that was the case.[2] In the United States, Donald Trump rose to power on a cascade of false and misleading claims about crime, trade, immigration, the economy, and other topics that—although they were identified as mistaken at the time—made very little difference to an enormous segment of the American populace who felt that they were true. Trump had barely been sworn into office before making a series of bogus claims that he had actually won the popular vote (although he had lost it by 3 million), that it was sunny rather than rainy during his inauguration speech (though witnesses disagreed), and that his inauguration had been the largest and best attended in US history (despite photographic evidence that clearly showed otherwise).[3]

All this is disturbing enough, as we contemplate the violence done to our customary norms of fact-checking and the standards for truth itself. With the ongoing assault on those professions that are committed to fact-based evidential reasoning—academics, the media, and intelligence gathering—one laments the erosion of our standards of truth and the subordination of epistemology to politics. Every time President Trump dismisses an accurate news story as "fake news" simply because it displeases him, further damage is done to the expectation that truth matters, either through consequences for politicians who lie, expectations of accountability in government, or the education of our electorate.[4] Without stretching it too far, one might say that we have already entered the "post-truth" era.[5]

What is less commonly appreciated, however, is that this campaign of doubt and disinformation—as part of a more general attack on liberal values—may be the first step toward the institution of authoritarian rule in the United States. One does not have to look too far in history, or too far across the globe, to see that assault on the norms of truth and against those who are truth tellers is a favored tactic of autocratic rulers, who wish to institute their own version of reality in order to facilitate their rule. As Jason Stanley explains in his insightful book *How Propaganda Works*, the point of propaganda is not necessarily to convince someone that what you are saying is correct, but to show that you have enough power to say something false without fear of challenge or consequence.[6]

In this chapter I explore the conceptual and historical roots of how the recent attack on truth in the United States may be exploited for political purposes and how those of us who are concerned about the values of liberalism can learn to fight back.

Authoritarian Worries

The Russian dissident Masha Gessen was one of the first to sound the alarm about the potential authoritarian consequences of post-truth. In a 2017 interview, she offered an important insight into why Donald Trump seemed so comfortable lying, even when he could easily be disproven. Trump does not lie because he believes what he is saying to be true—nor to change the minds of others—Gessen argues. Trump lies to assert power. "Every time [Trump] lies, especially when he lies about something really obvious—like the size of the inauguration—he's saying 'I can say whatever I want to, and there's nothing you can do about it.' I think he understands this instinctively."[7]

In this, Trump has learned the lesson of countless dictators and strongmen across the ages, a lesson that could well be taught by his opposite number in Russia, Vladimir Putin. Real power does not need the consent of the governed. One need not worry about changing others' beliefs (which may be thought of as requesting their cognitive consent) when one can merely dominate their reality.

The historical parallels for this sort of connection between an assault on truth and an assault on the liberal values that allow people to live freely are easy to identify. Writing about the totalitarian regimes of the 1930s, the eminent Holocaust historian Hannah Arendt once observed that "the ideal subject of totalitarian rule is not the convinced Nazi or the convinced communist, but people for whom the distinction between fact and fiction . . . true and false . . . no longer exist."[8] In the initial stages of an autocratic regime, it is not uncommon for a would-be ruler to see how many lies he or she can get away with, before pushing for more power, then ultimately solidifying that power through the institution of propaganda. As explained, the point is not persuasion but control. Contempt for truth goes hand in hand with political oppression.

What makes one think that this is the direction we are heading in the United States? If the alarm bells were going off merely for liberals, who were using historians like Arendt to make over-the-top comparisons between Trump and brutal dictators like Hitler and Stalin, perhaps this argument would not be taken seriously.[9] Once Trump took office, however, we saw a series of disturbing claims made by heavyweights in the governmental and journalistic arena, who are liberals and conservatives alike.

On CNN, on February 18, 2018, the political analyst David Gergen—a onetime adviser to Presidents Nixon, Ford, Reagan, and Clinton—had this to say:

We have an election that's just around the corner later this year. What if the Democrats, you know, take the House back? Are they all—is that all going to be blamed on fake news? What if they fall short? Are Democrats going to think, you know, it was all that meddling, and they [Republicans] have won a few seats that they wouldn't have otherwise won? This is what splits a country apart, and [in] many other countries it's the beginning of an authoritarian rule, and that's the larger threat hanging over us now. . . . [And I find] the threat is growing. There is this new book out about how democracies die written by two Harvard professors and it's quite striking . . . about the number of countries that were led by democratically elected leaders, but they turned more and more authoritarian. A dozen countries have flipped from democracy to authoritarianism since the end of the Cold War. We're not immune to that.[10]

A similar conclusion was drawn by E. J. Dionne, a Senior Fellow in Governance Studies at the Brookings Institution and a long-time columnist for the *Washington Post*:

When a leader who often praises strongmen abroad defines routine political opposition as disloyalty to country and then suggests hauling out the military to march in our streets as he looks down from on high, friends of freedom should take notice. Those who challenge portrayals of Trump as an authoritarian or an autocrat because our freedoms are still intact miss the point. In enduring democracies such as ours, liberty is eroded slowly by politicians who undermine the norms and practices that protect it.[11]

In her book *Fascism: A Warning*, former secretary of state Madeleine Albright openly worries that the United States may be at risk of heading toward one of the most heinous forms of authoritarianism—fascism. In so doing, she takes up the worry expressed by Sinclair Lewis and many others in the 1930s over whether "It Can Happen Here" in America. Albright's answer is that yes, it can:

[D]espots rarely reveal their intentions and . . . leaders who begin well frequently become more authoritarian the longer they hold power. . . . [W]hy, this far into the twenty-first century, are we once again talking about Fascism? One reason, frankly, is Donald Trump. . . . From the early stages of his campaign and right into the Oval Office, Donald J. Trump has spoken harshly about the institutions and principles that make up the foundation of open government. In the process, he has systematically degraded political discourse in the United States, shown an astonishing disregard for facts, libeled his predecessors, threatened to "lock up" political rivals, referred to mainstream journalists as "the enemy of the American people," spread falsehoods about the integrity of the U.S. electoral process, touted mindlessly nationalistic economic and trade policies, vilified immigrants and the countries from which they come, and nurtured a paranoid bigotry toward the followers of one of the world's foremost religions.[12]

Perhaps some will be tempted to dismiss these concerns as those of a partisan, since Albright worked in two Democratic presidential administrations. But then consider the following statement from a senior intelligence official who worked in both Democratic and Republican administrations and who comes to a similar conclusion.

Retired Air Force general Michael V. Hayden served as Director of the National Security Agency, principal deputy to the Director of National Intelligence, and as Director of the CIA under Presidents Clinton, Bush, and Obama. In his book *The Assault on Intelligence*, he makes several eye-opening statements about the dangers that post-truth can play in eroding the fabric of a democratic society:

> We in the intelligence world have dealt with obstinate and argumentative presidents through the years. But we have never served a president for whom ground truth doesn't really matter. . . . In this post-truth world, intelligence agencies are in the bunker with some unlikely mates: journalism, academics, the courts, law enforcement and science—all of which, like intelligence gathering, are evidence-based. Intelligence shares a broader duty with these other truth-tellers to preserve the commitment and ability of our society to base important decisions on our judgment of what constitutes objective reality.[13]

The dangers of this sort of abridgement of the role that intelligence gathering—and truth-telling in general—has played in supporting the type of nonauthoritarian, open society we hope to preserve in the United States are obvious. But just in case anyone missed it, Hayden closes the circle by quoting the brilliant and incisive book *On Tyranny* by Yale historian Timothy Snyder.[14]

Hayden writes:

> Timothy Snyder keeps coming back to the importance of reality and truth in his magnificent pamphlet-length book *On Tyranny*. "To abandon facts," he writes, "is to abandon freedom. If nothing is true, then no one can criticize power because there is no basis to do so." He then chillingly observes, "Post-truth is pre-fascism."[15]

The Assault on Liberal Values

There is no pre-defined set of "liberal values"; if one asked different people one would probably get different answers. In nearly any account of the core beliefs that make liberal democracy possible, however, there are two that would be on almost everyone's list: freedom of the press and the rule of law. If post-truth were truly a precursor to authoritarianism (and we were now in a post-truth era), one would expect an assault on both of these principles. In this section I show how post-truth has posed precisely such a threat.

How Accusations of Fake News Pose a Threat to Freedom of the Press

The problem of "fake news" is well known. It is not a new phenomenon (and surely goes back at least to the "yellow journalism" of the 1890s and probably before), but it has been in the news so much that people may think they know what it is, even if they do not. In my book *Post-Truth*, I had quite a bit to say about both the historical roots and insidious effects of fake news, with a particular focus on the problems that it created during the 2016 presidential election.[16] Here I wish to zero in on one of its more long-lasting collateral effects, which is the danger it poses to freedom of the press.

The role of fake news in influencing the 2016 presidential election in the United States is well known. As foreign meddlers and other parties created false and misleading content, then spread it on social media through Facebook and other platforms, the public became confused over what was true and what was false. Which sources were reliable? Who could be trusted anymore? As fake news stories competed with real news, we saw how easy it was to manipulate public opinion, and the terrible costs this had not only for trust in the media but also for the role that the press must play in providing the kind of accurate information that is the lifeblood of living in a free society.

Since the election, however, we have seen the term "fake news" picked up as a weapon against one's political opponents. During a press conference on January 11, 2017, even before he was sworn in as president, Donald Trump refused to take a question from CNN reporter Jim Acosta: "You are fake news." In February 2017, Trump tweeted that fake news was "the enemy of the American people." Later, after the press asked some particularly hard questions about his preparation for the North Korean summit, Trump tweeted "the Fake news, especially NBC and CNN [are] fighting hard to downplay the deal with North Korea. . . . Our Country's biggest enemy is the Fake News so easily promulgated by fools!"[17] This sort of attack on the mainstream press must be understood for what it is: a deliberate strategy to undermine the credibility of a press that sometimes reports information that is unflattering to the president. According to Jim Rosen, a journalism professor at New York University, "It's the erosion of the common world of fact. If we can't agree on what the facts are, if there are no facts because they are in endless dispute, there is no accountability."[18] As accusations of "fake news" are now being made against legitimate news organizations—with no compelling evidence that their reporting is biased or even inaccurate—we can come to no other conclusion than that the term has been hijacked for use against news coverage that goes against the president's interests.[19] In such an environment, the very idea of truth itself seems in danger of becoming partisan.

Here it is important to be clear about the definition of fake news. Fake news is not news that is merely false, but news that is *intentionally* false. In order to create fake news, one has to do so on purpose, with the goal of trying to get someone to believe something that is not true. In this sense, it is important to realize that just because a news story is *mistaken*, this does not mean that it is "fake." Legitimate news organizations occasionally make mistakes, or even share information that is false, but this is *not* the same thing as creating or sharing "fake news." In order for a news story to be fake, the people who created it would have to have the *intention* to mislead. They would have to be biased, underhanded, or have an agenda that is the journalistic equivalent of lying. There is a difference between *mis*information and *dis*information. Just as stating a falsehood is not a lie unless one knows it to be untrue, writing a news story that is false is not fake news unless its author does so with the intention to mislead.[20]

The fact that legitimate news organizations have a culture in which they are expected not only to follow good journalistic conventions—such as disclosing potential conflicts of interest, double sourcing information, fact-checking, *and then correcting any mistakes that may slip through*—suggests that what they are up to is *not* fake news. Even if one does not like what they say, neither this nor any occasional mistakes are sufficient for accusations of bias. In fact, in some ways one might say that it is the *job* of journalists to expose facts that are against the interests of those in power. As George Orwell once said, "Journalism is printing what someone else does not want printed; everything else is public relations." The job of the media is first and foremost to tell the truth.

This means that the *accusation* of fake news, when one knows or even suspects that such intentional dissimulation is *not* the motive, is *itself* a kind of fake news. To accuse journalists not merely of being inaccurate, but of being *intentionally* inaccurate, should carry a very high bar of proof. In fact, this amounts to saying that news organizations are engaged in a kind of conspiracy to betray the values that they have sworn to uphold. In light of this, I ask you to consider which is more likely: that there is a worldwide conspiracy of news organizations to obscure the truth about whether illegal border crossings have been down rather than up in the past decade; or whether the truth about this topic merely hurts the interests of those who are hurling accusations of "fake news" when a story does not serve their political interests. Of course—as we saw in the 2016 election—fake news *does* exist, and I do not suggest that it should not be taken seriously. But in this same vein we must flush out and run to ground any *false accusations* of fake news as *themselves* the source of precisely what they are accusing their opponents of.

There are two potential harms that may come from the existence of fake news. There is the well-known "disinformation" effect that can happen when someone creates a news story that is deliberately false, but there is also a "ricochet" effect of causing someone to doubt a story that is *not* false. The first problem is that fake news can compete for attention with real news, causing us to make our decisions about many factors in human life—including voting—on a fraudulent factual basis. But the second effect is that accusations of fake news can be used for the political purpose of getting us to be cynical that there actually *are* any truth tellers left in the world, because every source is biased. Sometimes doubt and confusion can be just as effective as getting someone to believe a lie.

This is a classic double effect. People can take fake news for real, but they can also take real news for fake. Both are harmful. Both can cause injury not just to the factual basis of our decisions, but also to the very values of truth, facts, and evidence that are necessary for the smooth functioning of a democratic society. Of course, there is a remedy for the first problem. We can attempt to verify the truth for ourselves. We can exercise skepticism, and put a higher premium on fact checking. We can do the hard work of ferreting out which stories are fake so that we can discount them.

But what about the second problem? What are our tools against this?

The most important thing we can do to fight against the second danger of fake news—that it can cause us to be distrustful even of legitimate news sources—is simply to be awake to its danger and the potential political motive behind it. And we must understand the stakes. The accusation of fake news where there is none is intended to have a pernicious effect on truth tellers, and this is normally done with a dark purpose.

It is in the interest of autocratic governments not just to lie to their citizens but to create a culture of demoralization and distrust where they may come to doubt the idea that there *is* any real distinction between truth and falsehood. In this way, the goal is not merely to mislead us, but to make us cynical. To make us doubt the truth even when it is in front of our faces. And this serves the interests only of those who have something other than the truth that they want to peddle to us, which is a tried-and-true precursor to fascism.[21]

Just look at where we are in the world today. Accusations of "fake news" made by political figures in Western democracies are parroted by dictators around the world, who want to use this to silence journalists who spread truthful information that threatens their rule. And sadly, there are many examples of journalists who have been imprisoned or even killed by regimes that are threatened by their truthful news coverage.[22] Why would someone do this? If we look at world history, we see that regimes have attempted to silence truth tellers *precisely because it preserves their power to be able to lie with impunity* to those who are being governed. As we have seen, perhaps such a government does not expect anyone to believe its lies. But to have the power to lie *and not to be challenged* is the mark of true power. In such an environment, accountability is at risk of being replaced by despotism.

I therefore think that the greater danger of fake news is not just the dissemination of falsehoods, but the ricochet effect whereby *false* accusations of fake news can be used to prepare the ground for a culture of lying that serves the interests of those who seek to mislead the governed. A populace that is cynical and dispirited is easier to rule than one that is skeptical and awake. As the American response to this "ricochet effect" has now devolved to include the consequence of threatening to rescind the broadcast licenses of those media outlets that the president would deem "fake news" and to "loosen the libels laws" against all media outlets, we see all too clearly the nature of the threat that post-truth poses for freedom of the press. The danger of the post-truth tactic of fake news is not merely one of violence to the truth, but toward the values that are necessary for the preservation of political freedom in a fair and open society.

How Attacks on the Credibility of the Special Counsel's Investigation Undermine the Rule of Law

It is ironic that some of the very same post-truth tactics (like the creation and dissemination of fake news)—that arguably were responsible for the outcome of the 2016 presidential election—were also used to undermine the credibility of Robert Mueller's special counsel investigation into Russian interference in that very election. The reason, however, is not really surprising. It worked the first time, so why shouldn't it work again?

Ever since the announcement of the special counsel's investigation into Russian interference into the 2016 presidential election—which included inquiry into any possible coordination with the Trump campaign—President Trump and his lawyers appear to have determined that final judgment in this matter would not be made as a matter of law but instead in the court of public opinion.[23] Thus, the same tactics that were allegedly used to manipulate public opinion during the election were also deemed effective in achieving the desired outcome during and after the Mueller investigation.

The goal seemed to be to undermine the credibility of any "truth claims" that came out of Mueller's report. On nearly every occasion that the Russia investigation was mentioned, President Trump called it a "phony witch hunt," the result of political bias. Never mind the number of indictments or guilty pleas achieved, the evidence discovered, or the pattern of facts that were revealed over time: if it could be shown that all of this was merely the "fruit of a poisoned tree," then perhaps the blowback on Trump and his presidency could be mitigated and he would survive without criminal indictment or impeachment.

In this, one notes a striking similarity to the strategy that has long been pursued by science deniers on topics ranging from climate change to the link between cigarettes and cancer: deny the facts, make accusations of bias, create a counter-narrative, and then push it relentlessly until there is such confusion that those on the sidelines do not know what to believe. By exploiting the well-known cognitive bias of the "illusory truth effect" (sometimes also known as the "repetition effect") and the sort of social pressure that can lead to conformity in beliefs as long as one's allies are going along (which can go by the shorthand "tribalism"), the goal seems to be to "manufacture doubt" where there is none, and suggest with little to no evidence that there is "another side to the story." This strategy helped Trump and his followers achieve three desired outcomes: (1) to influence public opinion, (2) to provide cover for future actions, including firings and pardons, (3) to prepare the ground for pushback against any inconvenient facts or conclusions revealed in the special counsel's report.[24]

In fact, Trump and his attorneys:
- claimed that the president cannot be criminally indicted.[25]
- claimed that the president cannot be subpoenaed or otherwise compelled to testify.[26]
- claimed that the president has unlimited pardon power, including the power to pardon himself and/or any of his associates, even if they would be material witnesses against him in a criminal adjudication.[27]
- pushed back against the idea that the president can possibly obstruct justice, because he is in charge of the Justice Department and all its investigations.[28]

All this suggests that the main objective of Trump and his legal counsel was to show that as president he was "above the law," with the only true check on his power being that of the impeachment power of Congress leading to removal from office.

Given this, Trump's strategy of putting political pressure on those members of Congress who would judge him in the event of impeachment—by whipping up public opinion in his favor—makes sense. By convincing enough voters that the special counsel's investigation was politically biased, he was able to remove any real accountability for his actions. By making his fellow politicians afraid of taking action against him, he was able to escape any real consequences for his actions in either the legal or political arena. Even if the Mueller report had uncovered numerous instances of criminal misconduct up to and including treason itself and led directly to impeachment, the Republican majority in the Senate would have refused to remove him from office (just as it refused on two later occasions). The result is a chief executive effectively exempt from oversight, paving the way toward authoritarianism and autocracy.

To say that all of this undermines the rule of law would be an understatement. One can only imagine the response of the framers of our Constitution to a situation where the powers of the federal government were able to be exercised based on the whims of a single person—no matter how popular—instead of the checks and balances meant to serve as a bulwark against the possibility of autocratic rule. By making our political system in this country beholden to the *feelings* of the electorate—with no real concern for whether the facts support any given policy or strategy—I fear that the day may come when, although we may continue to have elections and legislatures, we will have ceased to be a democracy. In doing so we will have given up one of the first principles of our republic, given to us by John Adams when he wrote that we should always seek to be "a government of *laws* and not of *men*."[29]

Trump's strategy was to claim that he did nothing wrong, that there was no collusion between his campaign and the Russians, and that the only thing preventing us from seeing this has been political partisanship by the left and a biased media. Here it is clear why Trump employed such a post-truth strategy, even if he knew it was based on fabrications and omissions, invented facts and outright lies; he did so to save his own skin. But why were so many voters ready to let him get away with it? Is it just that they were not paying attention? In his essay "The Illuminations of Hannah Arendt,"[30] the philosopher Richard Bernstein suggests a deeper motive. Responding to Arendt's observation that "the result of a consistent and total substitution of lies for factual truth is not that the lies will now be accepted as truth, and the truth defamed as lies, but that the sense by which we take our bearings in the real world—and the category of truth vs. falsehood is among the mental means to this end—is being destroyed," Bernstein recognizes the complex and sometimes corrupting power of alienation and resentment:

Many liberals are perplexed that when their fact-checking clearly and definitively shows that a lie is a lie, people seem unconcerned and indifferent. But Arendt understood how propaganda really works. "What convinces masses are not facts, not even invented facts, but only the consistency of the system of which they are presumably a part." People who feel that they have been neglected and forgotten yearn for a narrative—even an invented fictional one—that will make sense of the anxiety they are experiencing, and promises some sort of redemption. An authoritarian leader has enormous advantages by exploiting anxieties and creating a fiction that people want to believe. A fictional story that promises to solve one's problems is much more appealing than facts and "reasonable" arguments.[31]

As we saw earlier, to be able not just to fight the facts but to dodge them with indifference is the mark of a true autocrat. To impose a reality on the governed not because it is true but because one simply has the power to do so is a necessary step on the road toward an authoritarian victory in the United States.

A Look Back . . . and Forward

We now face the uncomfortable but absolutely necessary question of what can be done to prevent the nightmare scenario outlined in previous sections. In this, we should take note of both recent and twentieth-century history. The countries of Hungary, Poland, Turkey, Egypt, Venezuela, Thailand, and the Philippines have all shown recent signs of following the well-worn path from post-truth to autocracy.[32]

In Turkey, for instance, we have seen a quick slide from its first-ever direct election of a head of state in 2014 to outright authoritarianism. Through a series of reforms and changes in response to an attempted military coup, President Erdogan has consolidated his control over the military through a series of show trials, instituted several religious strictures into secular law (such as mandating that women wear headscarves in public), and made changes in the electoral system that effectively rule out any opposition.[33] As one commentator put it:

> At every step of the way, there was a way to excuse each of Erdogan's attacks on democratic institutions and to refuse to connect the dots. But after [the June 2018] 'election' the end result can no longer be in doubt: Erdogan mounted a sorry show of a popular plebiscite to invest himself with nearly plenipotentiary powers. Turkey is no longer a liberal democracy, or even an illiberal one. Like Russia or Venezuela, it is an electoral dictatorship. The facts speak for themselves. Since a failed coup in the summer of 2016, the Turkish state has jailed more than 300 journalists . . . and fired more than 100,000 state

employees it decried as 'enemies of the people.' Turkish state television has long since become a purveyor of pure government propaganda, and Erdogan's allies also control the vast majority of private media outlets. The leader of one opposition party had to campaign from jail, and protestors were often roughed up by the government's infamous security forces.[34]

In perhaps the most damning evidence of all, "Four days before the vote, the country's official news agency mistakenly shared the final election results with a government-friendly TV channel."[35]

Yet, as history shows, despite the seemingly omnipotent powers of an authoritarian regime to force its will, for a government to succeed in establishing these powers in the first place it requires the complicity (or at least passivity) of its people. As contemporary scholars on Germany in the 1930s have made clear, in works such as *They Thought They Were Free*[36] and *The Death of Democracy*,[37] the slide toward Nazism was abetted by the decisions of its citizens at crucial points along the way. And this can be gradual.

According to Aziz Huq, who studied the common properties of democracies and identified thirty-seven instances in which the quality of democratic institutions had declined so far in the twenty-first century, it does not even require a constitutional crisis. More often than not, authoritarianism these days comes not as the result of a military coup, but through a legal grab for power.[38]

> The road from democracy is rarely characterized by overt violations of the formal rule of law. To the contrary, the contemporary path away from democracy under the rule of law typically relies on actions *within* the law. Central among these legal measures is the early disabling of internal monitors of governmental illegality by the aggressive exercise of (legal) personnel powers. Often, there are related changes to the designs of institutions which might be brought about through legislation. Ironically, the law is deployed to undermine legality and the rule of law more generally.[39]

This has the startling consequence that many citizens may not notice that authoritarianism is creeping up on them. Those who resist by saying that the "illiberal" changes are all allowed by law, or that their institutions still survive, are missing the point. As the example of Erdogan's reelection in Turkey (and similar sham elections in Russia) clearly show, it is possible to live in a nation that allows one to vote, but that does not mean one lives in a democracy.

> Even in near-total autocracies, many of the institutions of democracy survive—in neutered form. . . . There need not be sharp inflection points. Indeed, it is worth reflecting on the fact that democracy is not a simple concept, but is instead both elusive and plural in practice. It relies on drams of transparency,

legality, impartiality, and constraint. These are promoted by a range of different laws, norms, institutions, and individual loyalties. All of these rarely vanish all at once. Their evaporation is ineffable and easily missed.[40]

As another commentator so aptly put it:

> For a democracy to exist and survive, you need more than the ballot box. You need rule of law, separation of powers, free and diverse media, independent academia, women's rights, minority rights and freedom of speech.[41]

Once a nation is on the path of eroding its democratic institutions, history warns that there may not be much time left. Power-hungry governments do not wait forever to consolidate their power. They poke and prod, seeing what they can get away with, before they seize an opportunity to expand their rule.[42] Are we perhaps one terrorist attack or Reichstag fire away from the next step down the road toward authoritarianism in the United States?[43]

According to Steve Schmidt, a former Republican operative, in the first two years of Donald Trump's presidency we witnessed a series of actions reminiscent of a pattern that has led to authoritarian rule in other countries:

> [Trump] doesn't believe in liberal democracy. And what we're seeing here every day are five behaviors. One, he incites fervor in a base through constant lying. Two, he scapegoats minority populations and he affixes blame for complex problems to them and them alone. Three, he alleges conspiracies that are hidden and nefarious and linked to those scapegoated populations. Four, he spreads a sense of victimization among those fervent supporters. And five, he asserts the need to exert heretofore unprecedented power to protect his victim class from the conspiracies and scapegoated populations. Through all of history, you understand in totalitarianism, you understand how democracies fall. You will find those five behaviors.
>
> Conservatism has become synonymous with obedience to the leader, a leader who says I am the law, I am above the law. I will define what truth is. Truth is what the leader says it is, not what we would have recognized months ago as objective truth. And so the Republican Party has become a threat to liberal democracy and all over the world. We see a regression in Poland, in Hungary, the rise of far-right ethno-nationalist parties and the last time this happened it unleashed a tragedy the likes of which the world has never seen. And I think there's a real lack of imagination in this country about how fragile these institutions are and about how dangerous a president as unprepared, as authoritarian, as ignorant as he is and the damage that he would be able to cause.[44]

With attacks on the press, criticism of the FBI and an independent judiciary, political rallies in which the press are kept in pens, criticism of our allies, embrace of dictators, threats to jail his political enemies, the tendency toward rewarding loyalty over competence, the avoidance of oversight or rule-following in those ethical and financial norms meant to prevent government corruption, and the appearance of what can only be thought of as "detention camps" for asylum seekers to this country—including young children—have we missed any of the warning signs that this road is leading somewhere?

What's next? Might a horrific crisis—either manufactured or organic—lead to martial law? The use of force against civilian dissent? Jailing of political dissidents? The suspension of elections?[45] If all these seem too frightening or unlikely in the United States, one is well to remember that *all* these tactics have been employed by autocratic governments across the globe and throughout history.[46] Indeed, we do not have to look back very far to see how in some societies this later culminated in political assassination, forced labor camps, and "ethnic cleansing." Surely we are not that far gone yet. Indeed, some may feel that it is insulting even to draw the comparison. But if we refuse to be awake even to the danger, will we know autocracy when it finally arrives? As Evan Osnos brilliantly observes in his *New Yorker* essay "When Tyranny Takes Hold," about his experiences with political repression in China: "What is the precise moment, in the life of a country, when tyranny takes hold? It rarely happens in an instant; it arrives like twilight, and, at first, the eyes adjust."[47]

Fighting Back

What might stop the United States from taking the next steps down this dark and dangerous road? In a cogent analysis of the threats that may soon be upon us, University of Iowa law professor Paul Gowder argues that the history of authoritarianism suggests two main lines of resistance:[48]

1. Coordinated civil opposition to any illegal government activities.
2. Continued efforts to expose and threaten the government's means of consolidating and exercising its autocratic powers.

He writes:

The first and most important tool to resist creeping authoritarianism is to refuse to succumb to . . . the impulse to conceal opposition to the administration out of fear of retribution. Opponents of the regime must have the courage to ignore the threats from pro-Trump thugs and motivated law-enforcement abuses *now*, when they're relatively mild. . . . The thing about the dispersed and coordinated resistance to political violence, hate crimes, and government overreaching is that it gets stronger with practice.[49]

Why is civil resistance so effective? Because would-be autocrats throughout history have depended on the passivity—if not outright complicity—of the larger population to get away with the sorts of abuses that may later become inevitable.

In an essay entitled "It Can Happen Here"—a review of two books about Hitler's Germany[50]—Cass Sunstein makes the point that most of the atrocities under the Third Reich built slowly over time, precisely because ordinary citizens did not see them in time to take sufficient steps to resist. Quoting from a first-person account quoted in Milton Mayer's book *They Thought They Were Free*, Sunstein shares the thoughts of one ordinary German citizen:

> We had no time to think about these dreadful things that were growing, little by little, all around us. . . . [We lived under] the gradual habituation of the people . . . little by little, to being governed by surprise.[51]

Others, of course, were probably intimidated from taking action for fear that they would get caught up in the consequences that grew from showing dissent. If those who showed resistance were randomly assaulted by police forces, this sent a double message: it demonstrated not only that dissenters were being punished, but reinforced the idea that no one would come to the assistance of any bystanders who might have considered getting involved. Others were simply distracted. Sunstein writes:

> [A] form of terror began quickly, as members of the SS made their presence felt, intimidating people in public places. At the same time, citizens were distracted by an endless stream of festivities and celebrations. The intimidation, accompanied by the fervent, orchestrated pro-Nazi activity, produced an increase in fear, which led many skeptics to become Nazis. Nonetheless, people flirted, enjoyed romances, 'went to the cinema, had a meal in a small wine bar, drank Chianti, and went dancing together.' . . . 'The automatic continuation of ordinary life . . . hindered any lively, forceful reaction against the horror.'[52]

In the end, Sunstein concludes that "habituation, confusion, distraction, self-interest, fear, rationalization, and a sense of personal powerlessness make terrible things possible."[53]

What is the alternative? In an article entitled "Will We Stop Trump Before It's Too Late," Madeleine Albright shares her prescription:

> What is to be done? First, defend the truth. A free press, for example, is not the enemy of the American people; it is the protector of the American people. Second, we must reinforce the principle that no one, not even the president, is above the law. Third, we should each do our part to energize the democratic process by registering new voters, listening respectfully to those with whom

we disagree, knocking on doors for favored candidates, and ignoring the cynical counsel: "There's nothing to be done."[54]

With an estimated five million people who participated in the "Women's Marches" in cities all across America in January 2017, an estimated one million who participated in the April 2017 "March for Science" in 600 cities around the world, and the tens of thousands who turned out in Boston and other cities in August 2017 for "Anti-Fascist" rallies in response to the "Unite the Right" rally that had taken place in Charlottesville the previous week, it is clear that many Americans have claimed a stake in resisting their government. With sit-ins at politician's offices and town halls, and spontaneous intervention at airports and at the border in response to Trump's policies that have targeted immigrants and Muslims, there is plenty of political action.

But there remains an important question. In the fullness of time, as Trump continues to lie to the American people—and various media outlets serve his agenda—will we become so inured to the tactics of post-truth that we no longer exercise the will to resist them? Worse, what will we do about the growing temptation to fight fire with fire, and engage in half-true or misleading information in service of a liberal agenda? Can we remain committed to supporting those truth tellers who expose the financial misdealings, public corruption, and abuses of power that can get lost under a cloud of post-truth, even if they sometimes cut against our own interests? And what shall we do about our fellow citizens who do *not* understand that when the Trump administration tells them that illegal border crossings are skyrocketing, or that illegal immigrants commit a higher proportion of crime than American citizens, they are lying? Perhaps the most effective resistance one can engage in to stop post-truth tactics from paving the way toward authoritarianism is not just physical but psychological. We must tell the truth, even if that means sometimes fighting the cognitive and ideological forces that may seduce us into avoiding it ourselves.

It is well known that Hitler's propaganda minister Josef Goebbels was a master at using the cognitive biases of "source amnesia" (forgetting where you heard something) and the "repetition effect" (believing something that you've heard over and over) toward the art of mass deception. If you can control the truth, you can control the population. Deception, manipulation, and exploitation are recognized tools in setting about to create an authoritarian political order. You do not need to force someone to do what you want if you can convince them to act on their own belief that it is true. But, by similar reasoning, if you can convince a population to be skeptical and think for themselves, perhaps the authoritarian threat can be avoided. A quotation widely attributed to Goebbels best captures the threat that post-truth poses for liberal values: "Propaganda works best when those who are being manipulated are confident that they are acting on their own free will."[55]

Postscript (June 2021)

This chapter was written during the darkest days of the Trump administration, before the election of 2020. After 30,000 lies,[56] widespread corruption, two impeachments, and a bobbled pandemic response that left more than half a million Americans dead, Joe Biden was elected president. So all is well, right?

Not hardly. As I write this, we are still in the depths of a partisan post-truth crisis in the United States, and it remains far from clear how things will turn out.

In the runup to the 2020 election, Trump famously said that the only way he could lose would be if the election were stolen from him and—wouldn't you know it—after the votes were counted, and recounted, and multiple state audits were performed that certified the fact that Joe Biden was the winner of both the electoral and the popular vote, Trump maintained that there was widespread voter fraud that had cost him the election.[57] Worse, Trump's "big lie" then metastasized its way throughout the Republican Party, which culminated in the January 6 insurrection at the US Capitol, incited by none other than President Trump himself.

History will record that on that day several thousand Trump supporters—many carrying Trump flags and "Stop the Steal" protest signs—laid siege to the Capitol building, just as the assembled members of Congress inside were voting to certify Joe Biden's election. The timing, of course, was not a coincidence. The crowd had been encouraged to do this in order to try to disrupt the vote, which they in fact did (at least for a few hours), in hopes of overturning the election and keeping Trump as president. In the process, hundreds of Capitol police officers were assaulted, a full gallows was erected on the Capitol grounds, armed thugs roamed the rotunda chanting "Hang Mike Pence!" and "Where's Nancy?" and various acts of vandalism and terrorism were committed. It is a miracle that all the elected officials and their families were able to flee and hide throughout the building without being physically harmed. Later that evening, election certification resumed *with 147 Republican members of the House refusing to accept the certified electoral count of the states*, thus seeking to overturn the results of a free and fair election and hand it to Trump.[58]

And all this happened before Biden had even been inaugurated.

Since then, the "big lie" has merely picked up steam, as the Republican Party has more or less imploded into a cult of personality for Donald Trump. Whether from fear or agreement, hundreds of Republican members of Congress continue to refuse to admit publicly that Biden won the election. Representative Liz Cheney (R-Wyoming) was stripped of her leadership post in the US House for stating the truth that Biden won the election and asserting the idea that the Capitol riots should be investigated. Soon after, Republicans in the Senate blocked the appointment of a bipartisan commission to investigate the January 6 insurrection because it might hurt their prospects in the 2022 midterm elections (or perhaps reveal some members' complicity in the assault). With such failure of leadership, it should come as no surprise that 70 percent of Republican voters think that the election was stolen from Trump.[59] In a later poll, 53 percent of Republicans said that Trump was still the true and rightful president.[60] Worst of all, fully 25 percent of Republicans have a favorable view of the cultish QAnon conspiracy theory, which predicted that a military coup in August 2021 would return Trump to power.[61]

Meanwhile, at the state level, GOP-controlled state legislatures have passed hundreds of voter suppression laws with an eye toward preventing anything close to the record election turnout in 2020. Texas even seeks a provision to make it easier for legislators to overturn a statewide election if they do not agree with the result. On top of gerrymandering, and a natural election cycle that often favors the out-of-power party at the midterms, such laws suggest that Republicans have an excellent chance of winning back the House of Representatives and the Senate in the 2022 midterms. And, if they do, who knows whether this time a GOP-controlled House might succeed in refusing to certify a Democratic winner of the 2024 presidential race, no matter the electoral outcome.

Could there be any clearer example of the danger of post-truth—or the threat it poses of authoritarian rule—than Trump's "big lie" and the Capitol riots he incited? If so, it would have to be the Republican Party's complicity in the six months that followed.

As I write this, one hundred historians and other experts in democracy have written a public statement warning that "history will judge what we do at this moment" because "our entire democracy is now at risk."[62] The dangers that Steven Levitsky and Daniel Ziblatt discuss in their 2018 book *How Democracies Die* are now more relevant than ever. As previously noted, in recent years democracies have fallen into autocracy all over the world. In early 2021, there was a military coup in Myanmar following a democratic election in which it was claimed—without evidence—that there was widespread voter fraud.[63] In response to a question about this situation, Trump's former national security advisor, General Michael Flynn, said that a similar coup "should happen" here too.[64]

The tactics of post-truth have preceded the path to repression and authoritarian rule in every instance we can name. This is a "break glass" moment for American democracy. Clearly, we are not out of the woods yet, even though we have a new president.

If the events of the last four years are not a threat to democracy—and a preview of what authoritarian rule might look like in the United States—what is? And it all starts with an assault on truth. With fake news. With disinformation and propaganda that are meant to condition a citizenry to believe a lie or accept an alternative reality, because that is what makes them feel important or keeps their side in power. To accept something as true because you *want* to believe it—that is the beginning of the "political subordination of reality," which is how I define post-truth.

Even though the bulk of this chapter was written more than three years ago, it could not be more relevant or more timely to our current situation. Trump may be out of office, but his "big lie" and the damage it wrought still lingers. Indeed, the man himself lingers. Trump is now threatening to run for president again in 2024. If he is successful—whether at the ballot box or by fiat from a Congress filled with his allies—what might happen next?

Democracies continue to fall all over the world. Indeed, the question we now face is the same one we faced during the Trump presidency: will we do enough to prevent the United States from being next?

Notes

1. "'Post-truth' Declared Word of the Year by Oxford Dictionaries," BBC News, BBC, https://www.bbc.com/news/uk-37995600, last modified November 16, 2016.

2. John Henley, "Why Vote Leave's £350m Weekly EU Cost Claim Is Wrong," *Guardian*, June 10, 2016, World, https://www.theguardian.com/politics/reality-check/2016/may/23/does-the-eu-really-cost-the-uk-350m-a-week.

3. Cleve R. Wootson Jr., "Donald Trump: 'I won the popular vote if you deduct the millions of people who voted illegally,'" *Washington Post*, November 27, 2016, https://www.washingtonpost.com/news/the-fix/wp/2016/11/27/donald-trump-i-won-the-popular-vote-if-you-deduct-the-millions-of-people-who-voted-illegally/?utm_term=.7d77c2eb4127; Jon Swaine, "Trump Inauguration Crowd Photos Were Edited after He Intervened," *Guardian*, September 6, 2018, World, https://www.theguardian.com/world/2018/sep/06/donald-trump-inauguration-crowd-size-photos-edited.

4. Indeed, it has now reached the point where Trump's usage of the term "fake news" to describe stories about him that are merely negative has rubbed off. As of January 2018, 42 percent of Republicans were willing to dismiss known-to-be accurate news stories as fake simply because they were negative about Trump. Erik Wemple, "Opinion: Study:

42 Percent of Republicans Believe Accurate—but 'Negative'—Stories Qualify as 'Fake News,'" *Washington Post*, January 16, 2018, Opinions, https://www.washingtonpost.com/blogs/erik-wemple/wp/2018/01/16/study-42-percent-of-republicans-believe-accurate-but-negative-stories-qualify-as-fake-news/?utm_term=.723079d6fce1.

5. In my book *Post-Truth* (Cambridge, MA: MIT Press, 2019), I define "post-truth" as the political subordination of reality.

6. Jason Stanley, *How Propaganda Works* (Princeton, NJ: Princeton University Press, 2015).

7. Denise Clifton, "Trump and Putin's Strong Connection: Lies," *Mother Jones*, October 19, 2017, https://www.motherjones.com/politics/2017/10/trump-and-putin-strong-connection-lies/; Lee McIntyre, "Why Donald Trump and Vladimir Putin Lie . . . and Why They Are So Good at It," *New Statesman*, January 3, 2018, https://www.newstatesman.com/world/2018/01/why-donald-trump-and-vladimir-putin-lie-and-why-they-are-so-good-it.

8. Hannah Arendt, *The Origins of Totalitarianism* (New York: Harcourt, Brace, 1951), part 3, chap. 13, para. 3.

9. Though note a recent poll jointly commissioned by the George W. Bush Institute and the University of Pennsylvania's Biden Center, which found that 50 percent of all Americans think the USA is in "real danger of becoming a nondemocratic, authoritarian country," with 37 percent of Republicans included in this figure. James Hohman, "The Daily 202: A Poll Commissioned by Bush and Biden Shows Americans Losing Confidence in Democracy," *Washington Post*, June 26, 2018, Analysis, https://www.washingtonpost.com/news/powerpost/paloma/daily-202/2018/06/26/daily-202-a-poll-commissioned-by-bush-and-biden-shows-americans-losing-confidence-in-democracy/5b318a5030fb-046c468e6f48/?noredirect=on&utm_term=.ef589f2e573c.

10. "Trump Links Shooting to Russia Probe; Trump's Media Allies in Denial," interview by Brian Stelter, *CNN Reliable Sources*, February 18, 2018, http://transcripts.cnn.com/TRANSCRIPTS/1802/18/rs.01.html. The book that Gergen refers to here is Steven Levitsky and Daniel Ziblatt, *How Democracies Die* (New York: Crown, 2018).

11. E. J. Dionne Jr., "Trump's Parade Plan Isn't Just Another Distraction," *Washington Post*, February 7, 2018, Opinions, https://www.washingtonpost.com/opinions/trumps-parade-plan-isnt-just-another-distraction/2018/02/07/132065ac-0c47-11e8-8890-372e2047c935_story.html?utm_term=.10d97bf2a128.

12. Madeleine Albright, *Fascism: A Warning* (New York: HarperCollins, 2018).

13. Michael V. Hayden, *The Assault on Intelligence* (New York: Penguin, 2018).

14. Timothy Snyder, *On Tyranny: 20 Lessons from the Twentieth Century* (New York: Tim Duggan Books, 2017).

15. Hayden, *Assault on Intelligence*, 187.

16. McIntyre, *Post-Truth*.

17. Donald Trump (@realDonaldTrump), Twitter, February 2017, https://twitter.com/realDonaldTrump/status/1006891643985854464?ref_src=twsrc%5Etfw%7Ctwcamp%5Etweetembed%7Ctwterm%5E1006891643985854464%7Ctwgr%5E363937393b70726f64756374696f6e&ref_url=https%3A%2F%2Fthehill.com%2Fhomenews%2Fadministration%2F392026-trump-calls-fake-news-the-countrys-biggest-enemy.

18. Ken Thomas, "Trump Tags US Media as Nation's 'Biggest Enemy' after Summit," *AP News*, June 13, 2018, https://www.apnews.com/f9614436c6364903af7f513ab72f8ddf.

19. After once (falsely) claiming that he had invented the term "fake news," Trump tends to use it to refer to stories about him that are negative rather than false. Phillip Bump, "Trump Makes It Explicit: Negative Coverage of Him Is Fake Coverage," *Washington Post*, May 9, 2018, Analysis, https://www.washingtonpost.com/news

/politics/wp/2018/05/09/trump-makes-it-explicit-negative-coverage-of-him-is-fake-coverage/?utm_term=.1a7de7eb35e7.

20. Some of the best examples of fake news come from the 2016 election, where Russian bots on social media created divisive posts meant to stir controversy. Scott Shane, "How Unwitting Americans Encountered Russians Operatives Online," *New York Times*, February 18, 2018, Politics, https://www.nytimes.com/2018/02/18/us/politics/russian-operatives-facebook-twitter.html.

21. Hannah Arendt, once again, makes the point: "In an ever-changing, incomprehensible world the masses had reached the point where they would, at the same time, believe everything and nothing, think that everything was possible and nothing was true.... The totalitarian mass leaders based their propaganda on the correct psychological assumption that, under such conditions, one could make people believe the most fantastic statements one day, and trust that if the next day they were given irrefutable proof of their falsehood, they would take refuge in cynicism; instead of deserting the leaders who had lied to them, they would protest that they had known all along that the statement was a lie and would admire the leaders for their superior tactical cleverness."

22. Jamal Khashoggi, "All You Need to Know about Saudi Journalist's Death," *BBC*, February 24, Europe, https://www.bbc.com/news/world-europe-45812399.

23. "Giuliani: 'Public Opinion' Will Decide Impeachment," *CNN State of the Union*, May 27, 2018, https://www.cnn.com/videos/politics/2018/05/27/sotu-giuliani-impeach.cnn.

24. Bob Dreyfuss, "Trump's All-Out Attack on the Rule of Law," *The Nation*, February 1, 2018, https://www.thenation.com/article/trumps-all-out-attack-on-the-rule-of-law/.

25. Johnathan Turley, "Giuliani Says Mueller Can't Indict but It Might Go Better for Trump if He Does," *Washington Post*, May 18, 2018, https://www.washingtonpost.com/news/posteverything/wp/2018/05/18/giuliani-says-mueller-cant-indict-but-it-might-go-better-for-trump-if-he-does/?utm_term=.1c07b32011bb.

26. Allison Frankel, "Experts Bash Giuliani Claim That Mueller Can't Subpoena Trump," *Reuters*, May 17, 2018, https://www.reuters.com/article/us-otc-mueller/experts-bash-giuliani-claim-that-mueller-cant-subpoena-trump-idUSKCN1II2XF.

27. Pat Ralph, "Giuliani Says Trump 'Probably' Has the Power to Pardon Himself," *Business Insider*, June 3, 2018, Politics, https://www.businessinsider.com/can-trump-pardon-himself-giuliani-says-yes-2018-6.

28. Aaron Blake, "Rudy Giuliani Makes a Big New Concession: A President Can Obstruct Justice," *Washington Post*, May 18, 2018, Analysis, https://www.washingtonpost.com/news/the-fix/wp/2018/05/18/rudy-giuliani-makes-a-big-new-concession-a-president-can-obstruct-justice/?utm_term=.252f7efad673.

29. "John Adams," *Wikipedia*, last modified August 4, 2021, 15:27, https://en.wikiquote.org/wiki/John_Adams.

30. Richard J. Bernstein, "The Illuminations of Hannah Arendt," *New York Times*, June 20, 2018, Opinion, https://www.nytimes.com/2018/06/20/opinion/why-read-hannah-arendt-now.html.

31. Bernstein, "Illuminations."

32. Max Boot, "Democracy Is in Crisis around the World," *Washington Post*, November 21, 2018, Opinion, https://www.washingtonpost.com/opinions/global-opinions/democracy-is-in-crisis-around-the-world-why/2018/11/21/ccb6423c-ecf4–11e8–8679–934a2b33be52_story.html?utm_term=.75c1de977f13.

33. Yascha Mounk, "Turkey's Warning," *Slate*, June 24, 2018, https://slate.com/news-and-politics/2018/06/turkeys-election-should-be-a-warning-to-every-democratic-country.html.

34. Mounk, "Turkey's Warning."

35. Omer Taspinar, "Turkey Takes a Big Step toward Nationalist Fascism," *Washington Post*, June 25, 2018, Opinion, https://www.washingtonpost.com/news/theworldpost/wp/2018/06/25/erdogan/?utm_term=.f397435e4e99.

36. Cass R. Sunstein, "It Can Happen Here," *New York Review*, June 28, 2018, https://www.nybooks.com/articles/2018/06/28/hitlers-rise-it-can-happen-here/.

37. Timothy Snyder, "How Did the Nazi's Gain Power in Germany?" *New York Times*, June 14, 2018, Nonfiction, https://www.nytimes.com/2018/06/14/books/review/benjamin-carter-hett-death-of-democracy.html.

38. Aziz Huq, "This Is How Democratic Backsliding Begins," *Vox*, May 15, 2017, https://www.vox.com/the-big-idea/2017/5/15/15632918/democracy-autocracy-comey-trump-fbi-russia-coup.

39. Huq, "This Is How."

40. Huq, "This Is How."

41. Nathan Gardels, "Authoritarianism Is Changing the Very Fabric of Society," *Washington Post*, June 26, 2018, Opinion, https://www.washingtonpost.com/news/theworldpost/wp/2018/06/26/turkey-election/?utm_term=.a12a8f7c5e5d.

42. Fintan O'Toole, "Trial Runs for Fascism Are in Full Flow," *Irish Times*, June 26, 2018, Opinion, https://www.irishtimes.com/opinion/fintan-o-toole-trial-runs-for-fascism-are-in-full-flow-1.3543375.

43. In "Turkey's Warning," journalist Yascha Mounk makes the argument that Turkey evolved from a democracy into an "electoral dictatorship" in just a few years. Yascha Mounk, "Turkey's Warning," *Slate*, June 24, 2018, https://slate.com/news-and-politics/2018/06/turkeys-election-should-be-a-warning-to-every-democratic-country.html.

44. "Supreme Court Upholds Trump Travel Ban," interview by Chris Hayes, *MSNBC*, June 26, 2018, http://www.msnbc.com/transcripts/all-in/2018–06–26.

45. In a recent poll, half of Republicans said they would support postponing the 2020 election if Trump proposed it. Ariel Malka and Yphtach Lelkes, "In a New Poll, Half of Republicans Say They Would Support Postponing the 2020 Election if Trump Proposed It," *Washington Post*, August 10, 2017, Analysis, https://www.washingtonpost.com/news/monkey-cage/wp/2017/08/10/in-a-new-poll-half-of-republicans-say-they-would-support-postponing-the-2020-election-if-trump-proposed-it/?utm_term=.50e96cca1383.

46. For instance, Russia, China, and Turkey.

47. Evan Osnos, "When Tyranny Takes Hold," *New Yorker*, December 11, 2016, https://www.newyorker.com/magazine/2016/12/19/when-tyranny-takes-hold.

48. Paul Gowder, "The Constitution and the Rule of Law," *Niskanen Center*, February 3, 2017, https://niskanencenter.org/blog/trump-threat-rule-law-constitution/.

49. Gowder, "Constitution."

50. Cass R. Sunstein, "It Can Happen Here," *New York Review*, June 28, 2018, https://www.nybooks.com/articles/2018/06/28/hitlers-rise-it-can-happen-here/.

51. Sunstein, "It Can."

52. Sunstein quotes from Sebastian Haffner, *Defying Hitler* (New York: Picador, 2003).

53. Sunstein, "It Can."

54. Madeleine Albright, "Will We Stop Trump Before It's Too Late?," *New York Times*, April 6, 2018, Opinion, https://www.nytimes.com/2018/04/06/opinion/sunday/trump-fascism-madeleine-albright.html.

55. Charles Simic, "Expendable America," *New York Review*, November 19, 2016, https://www.nybooks.com/daily/2016/11/19/trump-election-expendable-america/. It is important to note that some historians now dispute whether Goebbels actually said this.

56. Meg Kelly, Glenn Kessler, and Salvador Rizzo, "Trump's False or Misleading Claims Total 30,573 over 4 Years," *Washington Post*, January 24, 2021, Analysis, https://

www.washingtonpost.com/politics/2021/01/24/trumps-false-or-misleading-claims-total-30573-over-four-years/.

57. Over the next few months, when Trump and his lawyers took these allegations to court, they lost or had their lawsuits dismissed as "without merit" by over sixty courts, including some where Trump had appointed the judge. Trump won only one election lawsuit, which had nothing to do with allegations of fraud, and was later overturned by a higher court. https://www.politifact.com/factchecks/2021/jan/08/joe-biden/joe-biden-right-more-60-trumps-election-lawsuits-l/.

58. Karen Yourish, Larry Buchanan, and Denise Lu, "The 147 Republicans Who Voted to Overturn Election Results," *New York Times*, Updated January 7, 2021, https://www.nytimes.com/interactive/2021/01/07/us/elections/electoral-college-biden-objectors.html.

59. CNN, *Questions about Accuracy of Vote Counting Rise as Most Want to Vote before Election Day*, August 18, 2018, https://assets.documentcloud.org/documents/20694773/voting-and-elections.pdf.

60. "53% of Republicans View Trump as True U.S. President," *Reuters*, May 24, 2021, https://www.reuters.com/world/us/53-republicans-view-trump-true-us-president-reutersipsos-2021-05-24/.

61. Jason Lemon, *"A Quarter of Republicans Hold Favorable Views of QAnon Supporters: Poll," Newsweek*, March 18, 2021, https://www.newsweek.com/quarter-republicans-hold-favorable-views-qanon-supporters-poll-1577221.

62. Greg Sargent, "A Frantic Warning from 100 Leading Experts: Our Democracy Is in Grave Danger," *Washington Post*, June 1, 2021, Opinion, https://www.washingtonpost.com/opinions/2021/06/01/frantic-warning-100-leading-experts-our-democracy-is-grave-danger/.

63. Alice Cuddy, "Myanmar Coup: What Is Happening and Why?," *BBC News*, April 1, https://www.bbc.com/news/world-asia-55902070.

64. "Michael Flynn Appears to Endorse Myanmar-Style Coup in U.S.," interview by Dan Patterson, *CBS News*, June 1, 2021, https://www.cbsnews.com/video/michael-flynn-appears-to-endorse-myanmar-style-coup-in-u-s/.

CHAPTER 5

The New Conspiracism: Public and Private Harm and Immunity from the Law

NANCY L. ROSENBLUM

> This is the modern Lexington, this is the modern Concord. This is the modern fight where they're coming to take it all . . . it's an information war.
>
> —Alex Jones, *Infowars*[1]

> It's like a brushfire . . . if you leave it alone, it will burn down your forest, and it has reached all the way to the White House.
>
> —Leonard Pozner, Sandy Hook parent[2]

Conspiracism is nothing new in politics, but the conspiracism that has moved from the fringes of American life to social media and mainstream media and into the White House under President Trump is new. In *A Lot of People Are Saying: The New Conspiracism and the Assault on Democracy*,[3] Russell Muirhead and I assess conspiracist claims that strike at the heart of democracy: rigged elections, covert plots to impose martial law on Texas, charges that the political opposition is treasonous, the Department of Justice planning a coup. A conspiracist president imposed his compromised sense of reality on the nation. The flow of conspiracism through the capillaries of public life is constant. It has not abated with Trump's removal from the presidency.

The result is delegitimization of two foundations of liberal democracy: (1) the regulated rivalry of political parties with their acceptance of legitimate opposition and (2) knowledge-producing institutions. Conspiracism also causes personal disorientation, for it confounds what it means to know something and produces "epistemic polarization"—a schism among citizens that is arguably more unbridgeable and entrenched than partisan polarization. There is this, too: conspiracism targets individuals—inciting threats and violence.

In the first part of this essay, I identify features of the new conspiracism, its degradation of public life, and its cruel assault on private individuals. Conspiracy entrepreneurs target men and women personally and individually. And targeting comes from the top. President Trump leveled all-too-familiar conspiracist charges against innumerable officials and civil servants, and, memorably, at two women who opposed the appointment of Judge Brett Kavanaugh to the Supreme Court: they were not, he tweeted, what they seemed but "crisis actors" in the pay of some partisan political opponent.

In the second part, I discuss three efforts to contain and counter the new conspiracism. One is a classical liberal response—"speaking truth to conspiracy" and fact-checking. Another is the turn to defamation law by targeted individuals in an effort to restore their good name, exact retribution against their attackers, and deter further terrorization. Third, digital corporations have begun to censor or limit the spread of conspiracism that is rampant on their platforms; alongside this is the possibility of public regulation as remedy for the limitations of the industry giants' promised self-regulation.

So, do conspiracists inflict harms with impunity? Is the information terrain lawless? What measures against it are justifiable? The new conspiracism raises an old question—free speech and its limits—again.

The New Conspiracism: Degradation and Delegitimization

Pizzagate: Setting the Stage

The conspiracist concoction known as "Pizzagate" entered public life in 2016 and provides a concrete introduction to these themes. In outline, it charged that Hillary Clinton and her campaign manager, John Podesta, ran an international child-trafficking ring from the basement of a pizza parlor in northwest Washington, DC. Pizzagate emerged from the fringes when conspiracy entrepreneurs, including the Texas talk show host Alex Jones of *Infowars* and Fox News, spread the bizarre fabulation.

Calling Pizzagate a "hoax" discounts its gravity. For one thing, it shows that conspiracism on the internet generates real-world threats and material harms. James Alefantis, the owner of Comet Ping Pong, and his employees were threatened. Alefantis reportedly spent $70,000 on security guards and installed panic buttons in the restaurant. His business suffered.[4] Things got worse. Edgar Welch drove from North Carolina to the pizzeria and fired his semiautomatic rifle inside. Spurred by Jones's nonstop broadcasts, he had come to "self-investigate" and to rescue the children.[5] He found nothing, of course, not even a basement. Welch pleaded guilty to assault with a dangerous weapon and is serving a four-year prison sentence. Alex Jones "dissociated" *Infowars* from the story: "To my knowledge neither Mr. Alefantis, nor his restaurant Comet Ping Pong, were involved in any human trafficking."[6] The not-quite admission or apology has since been removed from the *Infowars* site.

Pizzagate is just one example of harm to private individuals. Another Jones follower was imprisoned after sending death threats to the father of one of the children murdered at Sandy Hook Elementary School.[7] Another blocked traffic on a bridge near Hoover Dam with a homemade armored vehicle.[8] Jones's conspiracy charge against a business retreat (Bohemian Grove) inspired a man to set a fire there, convinced that it was a site of human sacrifice.[9] The list goes on.

Pizzagate underscores the influence of conspiracy entrepreneurs, men (and some women)[10] who peddle assertions in return for money, celebrity, and influence. Jones's radio show—until recent legal actions against him—was broadcast on over 60 stations; before he was banned his YouTube channel had more than 2.3 million subscribers, and his videos had been viewed more than a billion times.[11] Conspiracism can be a lucrative business, and Jones markets supplements (Super Male Vitality, Alpha Power) and survivalist gear (Infidel Body Armor) along with alternative reality. But Jones wants more than profit. "I'm not a business guy, I'm a revolutionary," and true to form he "operates from behind bulletproof glass at an Austin industrial park ... with no identifying signs outside."[12] The new conspiracism comes from the radical political right and Jones is an extremist who seeks political influence; he wants his audience to repeat and amplify his charges online in what has become a distinct form of political participation. This is not lost on political candidates. Donald Trump appeared on his radio show in 2015 after launching his presidential campaign, gushing that "your reputation is amazing. . . . I will not let you down" and "we'll be speaking a lot."[13] "We advise the President," Jones claimed after Trump was elected, and "we've got the proof. Other people are scared to tell him what's going on."[14] Trump has repeated *Infowars* claims about illegal voters and media cover-ups of terrorist attacks. Jones called himself "the operating system of Trump": "I'm making it safe for everybody else to speak out just like Trump's doing."[15]

Entertainment and titillation fuel fabulations, but tribal politics is the root source of danger. Pizzagate makes narrative sense in a political context where the mindset that construes Hillary Clinton as so evil that nothing—not treasonous machinations to weaken the nation and not even sex trafficking in children—is beyond her. "Lock her up" and "Killary" signal that she does unthinkable things and that her abettors (Democrats, demon globalists, George Soros) conspire to cover them up. As digital platforms began to censor him, Jones insisted that he is the victim of a world-wide leftist cabal, and Trump echoes the charge that technology companies silence voices from the right.[16] Senator Ted Cruz declared Facebook's ban on Jones a "fascist assault on conservatives." In a ludicrous appropriation of Lutheran pastor Martin Niemöller's famous anti-Nazi poem, Cruz warned: "First they come for Alex Jones."[17]

Finally, Pizzagate shows that in a public atmosphere saturated with lies and disinformation, the new conspiracism is more than just one element in a dangerous stew. It is distinct and potent. Though Pizzagate began as the product of cynical conspiracy entrepreneurs, many conspiracist charges are perpetrated by people who claim to have unique insight into the fact that what appears to be true is not. They cast themselves as a cognoscenti with special knowledge. As I will show, confidence in their rightness matters to them and to their followers. Conspiracism is assented to by people for whom the apparently incredible story is "true enough."

Something else sets Pizzagate and other conspiracist claims apart: where even presidential lies are ephemeral—eclipsed the next day or often enough the same day by myriad other lies—and where many internet rumors "spike quickly and then fade out relatively quickly," conspiracy charges have a long half-life and "sustained participation."[18] Long after Alex Jones retracted his Pizzagate claims and removed his videos from circulation, the charge lived on. Protestors showed up at the White House on Saturdays with signs claiming that the news media is covering up child trafficking and demanding an investigation of Hillary Clinton.[19] On January 25, 2019, an arsonist set fire to the pizza parlor. Pizzagate spawned the current QAnon conspiracy to counter a conspiracy, and Q followers attend political rallies, police and elected officials wear the Q sign on their uniforms, and followers participated in the assault on the Capitol in 2021 to interrupt the certification of electoral votes. Intimidation is their business, until, that is, the promised "storm" led by Trump will eliminate all demons and enemies.

Jones and Pizzagate set the stage for identifying what this thing I call the new conspiracism is, its institutional consequences and epistemic effects, and the profound questions it raises of censorship, containment, and impunity.

What Is the New Conspiracism?

Both classic and new conspiracism exhibit with peculiar intensity a set of cognitive tendencies that are common to many people: the tendency to attribute important events to intentional agents, to look for proportionality between cause and effect, and confirmation bias. Beyond that, a quality of mind characterizes all conspiracists, classic and new: it dismisses challenging facts. So, for example, factual accounts of events from reliable sources are taken as evidence of the mainstream media's participation in the conspiracy,[20] just as documents released by government agencies or congressional committees are evidence of cover-ups. Transparency, the upside-down conspiracist argument goes, is itself a deception. In his analysis of the conspiracist mindset of American revolutionaries, Bernard Bailyn put it this way: "Once assumed [the picture] could not be easily dispelled; denial only confirmed it, since what conspirators profess is not what they believe, the ostensible is not the real, and the real is deliberately malign."[21]

In critical respects, however, the new conspiracism stands in contrast to classic conspiracy theory. We speak of "conspiracy theory" as if the two elements were inextricably linked. But the new conspiracism is *conspiracy without the theory*. We're familiar with conspiracy theories coming from the left and right around the 9/11 attacks on the World Trade Center, for example; they are intended to explain the incredible fact that nineteen individuals unaffiliated with any state, hiding out in a remote corner of Afghanistan, could successfully destroy the iconic buildings and attack the Pentagon. In insisting that the truth is not on the surface, classic conspiracism engages in a sort of detective work. Once all the facts—especially facts ominously withheld by reliable sources and omitted from official reports—are scrupulously amassed, a pattern of secret machinations emerges. The dots are woven into a pattern and a comprehensive narrative of events. Warranted or not (and some conspiracist claims are true, of course), classic conspiracism is conspiracy with a theory.

The new conspiracism is at the other extreme from the accumulation of evidence and exhaustive argument. It dispenses with the burden of explanation. Often enough there is no event to explain. Pizzagate is conjured out of thin air. No one reported children being smuggled into the restaurant. No cries were heard. No predators were spotted. With the new conspiracism there is no punctilious demand for proof.[22] There is no exhaustive amassing of evidence, however implausible, no dots revealed to form a pattern, no documentation of a long train of abuses all tending the same way, no close examination of the operators plotting in the shadows. Instead, the new conspiracism takes the form of bare assertion: "Rigged!"—just one word casts election results as manipulated.

What validates the new conspiracism is not evidence and argument but repetition. If *a lot of people are saying* it, it is true enough. Asked whether George Soros was secretly funding the "caravan" of migrants trekking toward the US border, President Trump replied, "I wouldn't be surprised. A lot of people say yes." At a New Hampshire campaign stop in September 2015, Trump was asked about Muslim communities operating military camps in the United States to prepare to conduct terrorist raids. Notwithstanding the absence of any evidence, he stoked the fear: "You know, a lot of people are saying that, and a lot of people are saying that bad things are happening out there."[23] Repetition affirms the now-ex-president's compromised sense of reality. What matters is the number of re-tweets his post enjoys. Forwarding, re-posting, re-tweeting, and "liking": these are how accusations are validated. And affirmation of conspiracist claims has become a form of political participation.

Senators Cruz and Hawley used nothing more than the fact of repetition to justify their attempt to overturn the electoral college vote. They did not cite a single example of irregularity but simply declared, "By any measure, *the allegations* of fraud and irregularities in the 2020 election exceed any in our lifetimes." A lot of people are saying the vote count was "rigged!"

The bar for assent to the new conspiracism is low: if something could have happened, even if there is no evidence for it at all, then it is true enough.[24] There's the "just asking questions" formula: "I would love to know more, but what I know is troubling enough." Hostile intent and capacity to commit the subterfuge make it true enough. Consider the White House press secretary's response to questions about Trump's tweet of a video that falsely purported to show a Muslim migrant committing an assault: "Whether it's a real video, the threat is real."[25] Because the world is one in which the claim could have been true, it is true enough. Here's what "true enough" sounds like: Congressman Bryan Zollinger, a Republican from Idaho, when asked about the allegation that Democratic Party officials had lured white nationalists and antifascist protesters to Charlottesville in 2017 in order to manufacture a violent clash, responded: "I am not saying it is true, but I am suggesting that it is completely plausible."[26]

Assent to the new conspiracism signals group affinity, or what has come to be called "tribal" belonging. People affirm a charge of secret, nefarious intent because it fits with the affinities, connections, and hostilities that comprise their political worldview and have become elements of personal identity. Assent is affirmation of identification with others who accept this compromised reality as true enough and who do not want to disassociate from the larger political narrative of covert cabals by elusive political enemies. Assent takes conspiracism out of the domain of individual psychology and into politics. A 2017 poll found that 47 percent of Republicans believed that Trump had won the popular vote, and about half of self-identified Republicans said they believe that American elections are "massively rigged."[27] The same conspiracist charge was made daily leading up to the 2020 election. According to a Reuters/Ipsos poll in the spring of 2021, 61 percent of Republicans believe that the election was stolen, and 53 percent believe that Trump is currently the true president.[28]

At its most intense, the new conspiracist appeal coming from the halls of power combined with social media bubbles adds up to a capacity for something like milieu control. This capacity to propagate a compromised version of reality drives many to advocate containing or regulating or censoring the flow of conspiracism; I turn to this below.

In his seminal essay *The Paranoid Style in America Politics,* Richard Hofstadter described the classic conspiracist paranoid style as a threat to what he saw as the moderate and pragmatic requirements of liberal democracy. The anti-Masonic and McCarthyite groups he studied, among others, rejected mediation and compromise and are averse to "the manner of working politicians."[29] Yet this description is not unique to conspiracists—it marks partisan extremists as well, political "purists." My point is that Hofstadter could not have foreseen the present partisan polarization that afflicts mainstream politics. He could not have anticipated the scope of new conspiracist assaults on liberal democracy. The damage extends far beyond moderation and pragmatic democratic practices—"the manner of working politicians." With their claims of rigged elections or a Justice Department coup d'etat or a treasonous Democratic opposition, they delegitimate democracy's foundational institutions.

Nor could Hofstadter have foreseen the shape the conspiracism would take—the bare assertion and innuendo and "just asking questions." For his classic conspiracists mimicked the methods of science and scholarship; as he described, warranted or unwarranted they were intent on collecting evidence, seeing patterns, making arguments—that is, offering explanations. The new conspiracism's source of validation—repetition and assent—produces, as Hofstadter's conspiracy-minded researchers did not, widespread "epistemic polarization" at the level of what it means to know something.

Epistemic Polarization

The content of new conspiracist charges is typically illiberal and antidemocratic, but content is not the only element of its assault on liberal democracy. There is also its corrosion of both knowledge and skepticism.

Skepticism and knowledge go hand in hand. A Millian orthodoxy has it that even when we are persuaded that, all things considered, the available evidence and argument point in a certain direction, we should be alive to the possibility that in spite of our best effort to get it right, we got it wrong. Our assurance of being right relies on doubt and an iterative process of self-correction. Assessing conspiracist claims, like everything else, requires willingness to entertain new information as it emerges from a plurality of sources. It entails a capacity to recognize that certainty is provisional. It requires, again, a capacity for self-correction.[30] It is inseparable from the virtue—both intellectual and political—of skepticism. In democracy it requires not only personal openness but a degree of public respect for knowledge and for reasonable doubt.

A plurality of knowledge-producing sources is the necessary resource for both knowledge and skepticism. The wealth of specialized knowledge, of science and social science, and of ethical perspectives provide the terrain from which we consider not only when our best understanding of facts and theories and explanations is limited or flawed but also when experts are wrong, when science is incomplete, and when reasons match or don't match the values we bring to politics (and everything else). When the pluralist bases of knowledge are closed down, when sources are delegitimized and thrust outside the orbit of consideration, when conspiracist transmitters have lost the capacity for receiving, the framework of questioning and assurance is undone.

That is the situation today as conspiracists stubbornly assert and reassert "both demonstrably false claims *and* unsubstantiated beliefs about the world that are contradicted by the best available evidence and expert opinion."[31] More, they directly assault knowledge, beginning with rejection of particular facts like the existence of Barack Obama's official birth certificate, and culminating in denial of the authority of the universe of institutions we depend on to produce specialized knowledge, expert judgment, and reliable communication.

This assault on knowledge-producing institutions follows on decades of charges of partisan bias and the creation of ideologically warring research centers, publications, and media. But conspiracists take things further. "Fake news" is more than a label applied to coverage that is deceptive or biased. It is an accusation of conspiracy, conveying that the mainstream media is "scum," colluding to disempower Trump and all real Americans and to weaken the nation: "They have their reasons, and you understand that."[32] As one penitent conservative lamented, the price of rejecting mainstream reporting "turned out to be far higher than I imagined. The cumulative effect of the attacks was to delegitimize these outlets and essentially destroy much of the right's immunity to false information. We thought we were creating a savvier, more skeptical audience. Instead, we opened the door for President Trump, who found an audience that could be easily misled."[33]

So it is striking that conspiracists turn the tables and embrace the notion that *they* are the real critical thinkers. For some time, literary scholars have offered up a romanticized characterization of conspiracism as a welcome, destabilizing disposition. Conspiracism, the argument goes, "disrupt[s] complacent, consensual, transparent theories of politics" and involves us "in a reiterative back-and-forth that mobilizes doubt and reassurance. . . . The narrative pivot . . . involves the step away from belief and into skepticism."[34] Conspiracists adopt this characterization, insisting that their radio shows and internet sites and videos are teaching information consumers to be questioners, to be "citizen journalists," to get all the facts and make up their own minds—as did the armed conspiracist who turned up at the pizzeria in Washington, DC, ready to self-investigate the child sex ring.[35] Advancing his fabulation that the murder of children at Sandy Hook was staged, Alex Jones says, "So, if children were lost at Sandy Hook, my heart goes out to each and every one of those parents. And the people who say they're parents that I see on the news. The only problem is, I've watched a lot of soap operas. And I've seen actors before. And I know when I'm watching a movie and when I'm watching something real."[36] Jones cast himself as the skeptic. He wanted to "open a dialogue" with the families because government and the mainstream media were misrepresenting things: "The idea they're pushing is that you can't ever question anything. . . . I don't think you can establish that anything is 100 percent fact."[37]

The conspiracist claim to skepticism is fraudulent. Conspiracists see challenges from mainstream media and official sources as an occasion for *reaffirming* their certitude. Here is a subscriber to the fantastical QAnon conspiracy talking to a fellow Q about family and friends who dismiss them as demented or simply bizarre: "You have to remember it's brainwashing. Think of it as an illness. I know it's hard not to get angry in the moment, but don't stay angry. You've woken up, you have to be patient and willing to . . . help them wake up." (By giving them what QAnons call "the red pill.")[38] Conspiracy followers are the cognoscenti who know things are not as they seem. They have esoteric knowledge of how things really are. They ask, "Who do you trust?" Consider the significance of this question: when we decide what community is worthy of epistemic trust, we are implicitly also deciding what it means to know something.

The result of this dual attack on knowledge and skepticism is epistemic polarization, which goes beyond divergent accounts of political reality. We are in a moment when some inhabit a world in which their common sense tells them it is absurd to suppose Hillary Clinton and her campaign chief are operating an international child sex ring and in which others find that plausible. There is no translation bridge connecting this divide. It fractures the common social and political world. There can be no politics—no argument or negotiation or compromise *or even disagreement*—which all require a shared horizon of knowledge and skepticism. What responses have been brought to bear on the conspiracist claim to own reality?

What Can Be Done?

Speaking Truth to Conspiracy

Attempts to contain conspiracism and its effects take a variety of forms, among them speaking truth to conspiracism, private legal action, and actions taken by the giant digital corporations. Each is supported by good reasons, yet each has problems that are familiar from historical and contemporary discussions of freedom of speech. Containing conspiracism carries twin dangers: that it will be too efficacious and chill speech or force it underground, and that it will not be effective enough.

The first response to conspiracism is the enduring liberal imperative to speak truth to conspiracy. But who rebuts and rebukes Jones's assault on the father of a child murdered at Sandy Hook as an actor pretending grief in order to promote gun control? Who speaks out against the president's claim that a "caravan of migrants" at the southern border is an invasion of terrorists and rapists funded by George Soros?

Strikingly, private individuals targeted by conspiracists are stepping out themselves to speak truth to conspiracy. Leonard Pozner, father of six-year-old Noah murdered in the Sandy Hook massacre, created a website to stop harassment and terrorization of the victims of this tragedy. He posts news articles on how to fight conspiracists, organizes volunteers to hunt down conspiracist content, and works to get media platforms to shut down these sites: "The very fact that Jones has some semblance of influence over our president's thinking speaks to my position that we should challenge his warped and pernicious views out in the open public forum."[39] Victims speaking out garner attention and raise awareness of conspiracism's immediate, personal harm. But except for legal cases that get local media attention, these messages reach only a limited, sympathetic audience.

Speaking truth also belongs to those inside and outside government whose authority derives from special knowledge. Thus, scientists and civil servants educate, advocate, and mobilize on climate change and a lot more. They embrace the role of "witnessing professionals," or should.[40] And civil society groups, especially advocacy groups, speak truth to conspiracy as a regular part of their work, for example, calling out fear-mongering conspiracist distortions against immigrants amounting to group libel.

The media, of course, is the institutional bulwark against conspiracist charges—the *sine qua non* of speaking truth. The capacity of officials and citizens to dispute conspiracist claims depends on arduous reporting using credible sources, and on a journalistic ethic that resists identifying its responsibility with "balance" and substitutes verifiability and accountability.[41] Fact-checking and exposing media and social media misinformation has become a distinct newsbeat.

The impact of fact-checking in the media and on digital platforms is under study, and there is no consensus among political psychologists and communication experts. For example, Brendan Nyhan reports that in experimental studies, when Facebook labels a headline "disputed," it turns out to be a weak counter; indeed, the presence of "disputed labels" causes study participants to rate unlabeled false stores as slightly more accurate—an "'implied truth' effect." Similarly, general warnings to "remain skeptical" reduce the perceived accuracy of news articles that were not false.[42] There is a growing literature on the so-called "continued influence effect" of misinformation even after correction and on the "backfire effect," which says that under certain conditions correction entrenches misinformation.

Specific difficulties plague fact-checking and correcting new conspiracist claims more than they do disinformation and lies. Charges that take the form of bare assertion or innuendo or just asking questions are elusive—there is no evidence to contradict, just as hateful racist elements of a charge are not rebuttable matters of fact. The evidence is mixed, then, but fact-checking and correction by the media are morally necessary.

As important as these efforts to speak truth to conspiracism are, elected political representatives are, or should be, the first line of offense against conspiracist claims precisely because conspiracism today has what I call a "partisan penumbra." There is an alignment between conspiracism and extremism housed in the Republican Party. Representatives' partisan connection gives them a degree of credibility and authority with their voters. It makes them trustworthy sources. Elected representatives have the responsibility of their office to bat down conspiracist claims; they have the advantage of influence; they draw media attention; they have the capacity to be listened to and heard by constituents and others. They are the most likely to reach and bolster and rally those who do not already have an entrenched conspiracist mindset.

When only a handful of Republicans breaks ranks with conspiracists in their party and with the conspiracist president, even today—when they fail to disrupt the exacerbated polarized dynamic that is now epistemic as well as political—the party explicitly or implicitly accepts conspiracist charges. Take, for example, the summer military training exercise called Jade Helm 15. Some Texans came to believe that the United States Army was plotting to invade the state, and Alex Jones fertilized such fears with his insistence that the army planned to disarm the population and impose martial law.[43] Leaders like Greg Abbott, the Republican governor of Texas, did not try to calm popular fears or resist conspiracist delusions with reasonable explanations based on their knowledge of events. Instead, officials signaled that they, too, had concerns. Abbott went so far as to task the Texas State Guard with monitoring the military operation on behalf of the state: "During the training operation," Abbott wrote to the guard, "it is important that Texans know their safety, constitutional rights, private property rights and civil liberties will not be infringed."[44] Republican officials in federal and state government have nearly unanimously subscribed to the "Big Lie."

Finally, to be clear, no amount of correction or remonstration is likely to be effective against those who assent to and spread conspiracist fabulations. Reasons both cognitive and tribal militate against changing their mindset or their allegiance. Put simply, they are transmitters, not receivers. This consideration lay behind a proposal by law professors Adrian Vermeule and Cass Sunstein for reaching the "hard core" holders of false beliefs. They suggest government infiltration of conspiracist groups. "Planting doubts" and "introducing beneficial cognitive diversity" are their prescriptions for repairing extremists' "crippled epistemology." Government, on this view, should attempt to "debias or disable its purveyors" in this fashion.[45] The proposition recalls J. Edgar Hoover's counterintelligence program, which infiltrated civil rights groups,[46] and, like Hoover's, appears to be a violation of civil liberties when the group is not a terrorist cell or violent association. In any case, the new conspiracists are generally not members of face-to-face extremist groups but are digitally dispersed across the world. Anyone is free to participate in the online creation and spread of conspiracy claims. Were the government to infiltrate such discussions on social media—and we now see that this has indeed been done by a hostile foreign government, using a variety of camouflages—the effort would sooner or later be exposed. The result would affirm the conspiracism it intends to combat.

So speaking truth to conspiracy aims first of all at reaching open (albeit baffled and disoriented) minds, not persuading conspiracists themselves. Here, too, difficulties emerge. One is information overload. The staggering frequency and velocity of conspiracist charges makes the need for response incessant. It is fatiguing. It can wear out both those who are challenging conspiracism and citizens who valiantly try to keep up. The difficulty of capturing public attention also owes to asymmetry: conspiracy without the theory deals in soundbites: "rigged!" and "hoax!" It is easy to state, spread, and swallow. In contrast, examination of concocted claims and fact-checking are the opposite of catchy and exciting: "The debunk seldom travels as far as the conspiracy claim and, indeed, it can help keep the claim conspicuous."[47] This recognition has shaped defamation law, where judges regularly observe that "denials, retractions, and corrections are not 'hot' news, and rarely receive the prominence of the original story," and "the truth rarely catches up with a lie."[48]

In short, the sufficiency of answering speech with more speech is being questioned—as indeed it always has been. It does not deter and may not do a lot to contain conspiracism. Yet over time it can weaken its impact. Speaking truth to conspiracism proceeds instance by instance, moment by moment, and open-minded citizens develop a cumulative awareness of conspiracism's force and harmful effects. It reorients those who are disoriented and buttresses citizens in their resistance. Also, the degradation of public life is measured, documented, recorded for analysts and historians. Speaking truth to conspiracism is a moral and political imperative. It provides assurance to people disoriented by conspiracism's claim to own reality and epistemic polarization that common sense notions of what it means to know something still hold. And it offers a sort of comfort to conspiracism's individual victims.

Individual Harm and Civil Remedies: Defamation

We know that First Amendment protection does not extend to fighting words, incitement, credible threats, and sometimes group libel, but most conspiracist claims, like Alex Jones's, don't fall into these categories. His charge that the parents of children murdered at Sandy Hook are really "crisis actors" have not been judged incitement of "imminent lawless actions," although people provoked by his rants have been convicted for threatening the Sandy Hook parents in a way that would reasonably cause fear for their safety. Jones was sanctioned in trial court for saying to Sandy Hook families' lawyers in a 2019 broadcast, "If you want blood, you've got it. Blood on the streets, man"—though not as incitement but as endangering the administration of justice.[49] Undeterred, Jones was connected to the January 6 insurrection. Incitement is the domain of criminal prosecution, and given the vast dimensions of enflamed conspiracism, threats, and encouragement of violence—most recently threats directed at electoral officials doing their jobs—legal charges are surprisingly rare.

Victims are exploring another route: the civil law of defamation. When Leonard Pozner, father of Noah, a victim of murder at Sandy Hook, successfully petitioned to get YouTube to remove an *Infowars* broadcast, Jones retaliated by revealing Pozner's personal information and maps that identified his family's addresses. Lucy Richards, a follower of Jones, left violent voice messages and email threats: "You gonna die, death is coming to you real soon."[50] Other Sandy Hook families suffered threats and on-line abuse, were videotaped and harassed, and some moved to a gated community with twenty-four-hour security.[51] Monuments to slain children in Newtown were stolen and defaced. All this in response to Jones's repeated story that there was no mass murder, that there was no shooter identified by the police as Adam Lanza, that the shooting was a false flag attack . . . and the conspiracy was the work of "government-backed gun grabbers."[52] In continuous broadcasts over many years the parents were called "Sandy Hook Vipers," liars, and frauds. The families sought a public accounting of the suffering they had endured, and that continues today.

Defamation law holds out the possibility of vindication, a public acknowledgment of harm, and deterrence of other conspiracists. When three children assaulted a five-year-old girl, Jones claimed that the attackers were from refugee families and involved Syrians, rape, and urinating in the victim's mouth, and he linked them all to Chobani: "Idaho Yogurt Maker Caught Importing Migrant Rapists." Jones settled a defamation suit with Chobani's owner, Hamdi Ulukaya.[53]

Sandy Hook families have brought a set of lawsuits for defamation and intentional infliction of emotional distress in Texas and Connecticut. The suits are a window onto the limitations of legal redress in this age of costless propagation of venomous claims.

Predictably, Jones mounted a First Amendment defense: "The lawsuit is a strategic device used by Plaintiffs to silence Defendants' free speech and an attempt to hold Defendants liable for simply expressing their opinions regarding questioning the government." The families are going after him for exposing government lies and cover-ups, the argument goes. Their political aim is to silence "an ardent and vocal supporter of the Second Amendment."[54] Jones adds a freedom of association argument: he is enlisting others to defend the Second Amendment, and the motivation behind the defamation suit is fear of his influence in public debate. It is, he argues, a classic "strategic lawsuit against political participation." Jones the conspiracist claimed that the families are part of a conspiracy against him.[55]

The families deny that their case involves political disagreement; it is a question "of just how much damage we're prepared to let a madman inflict on the lives of innocent victims through malicious lies and willful harassment."[56]

One thing is clear: the standards developed in defamation suits against traditional media do not apply well to the new technology and the new conspiracism. Jones tries to qualify as a news reporter and *Infowars* as a media outlet so that he can claim the standard of protection from liability established in *New York Times v. Sullivan* (376 U.S. 254, 1964). The protection extends to attacks on public figures—men and women of fame or notoriety in the community who presumptively sought the status of figures in the public eye. And *Rosenbloom v. Metromedia Inc.* (403 U.S. 29, 1971) extended the *New York Times* privilege to defamation of private persons if they are linked to "matters of public concern." In the 1974 case, *Gertz v. Robert Welch Inc.* (418 U.S. 323), Justice Lewis Powell limited "public figure" to those who consciously seek out that status. The purpose was to provide legal recourse for individuals who have not voluntarily exposed themselves to risk of injury from defamatory falsehoods and who have less effective opportunities for rebuttal than public officials and public figures.[57] Yet the door was left open a crack by offering traditional media protection from claims by "involuntary limited-purpose public figures," people thrust into the public debate by outside design. The presumption was that the status of "involuntary public figure" would be exceptional, and the protection granted media rare. That has changed.

The defamation charges against Jones revolved around the mass school shooting, an indisputable issue of public interest, but are the parents public figures? Jones argues that Pozner's participation in public debate to advance the agenda of gun control assigns him the status of public figure. Indeed, "public figure" has recently been interpreted to apply to status within very specific social contexts: "In the digital world, you can be a public figure in the contest of a particular videogame.... Even if no one outside that community would have heard of you."[58] On this view, the Sandy Hook parents could be called public figures in the gun control community or the conspiracist community. The point is that conspiracist charges today can create public figures instantly and virally. As Emma Grey Ellis writes in *Wired*, the *Gertz* decision assumed that becoming an involuntary public figure would be rare. "Not so in the age of the web. Having a mob of conspiracy theorists pillory you for articulating grief over a murdered child seems exactly the sort of public entrance no one would make voluntarily—and in an age of virality, such situations aren't even uncommon. We are all one rogue tweet away from public figure-dom."[59]

The new conspiracists' faux skepticism and charges in the form of innuendo and "just asking questions" also come into play. Jones's attorneys argue that his use of innuendo is something that is "not readily understandable" and therefore cannot be translated into a defamatory statement. That is, because his conspiracy charges are not really statements, they cannot be demonstrably false. Alternately, because demonstrably false statements about the Newtown parents seem unarguable, Jones's defense also appeals to a convoluted, protective Texas Supreme Court opinion: "Even when a statement is verifiable as false, it does not give rise to liability if the 'entire context in which it is made' discloses that it is merely an opinion masquerading as a fact."[60]

There are other twists. Jerry Falwell lost his defamation suit against *Hustler* magazine when the Supreme Court ruled that a parody advertisement claiming he had incestuous relations with his mother was so obviously ridiculous and clearly not true that nobody would believe that the defendant was serious or that the ad should be taken seriously. *Hustler* escaped liability. Would any reasonable person take Jones's claims about Sandy Hook parents as crisis actors seriously? Apparently, many did. What is the reasonableness test here?

Piling twist on twist, in a child-custody battle with his ex-wife Jones argued that his conspiracism and threats of violence should not be material evidence in evaluating his parenting. There, he represented himself as a performance artist, playing a character, acting the part of a conspiracist.[61] "Alex Jones does not in fact believe that the Sandy Hook shooting was a hoax—and never has." But does that make his story malice and reckless disregard or art? A humorist's list of guidelines for social media users captures this absurdity: "All Twitter users must now check a box indicating whether they're a white supremacist or a comedian. It will just be easier that way."[62] The play of opinion/statement/art/artifice is jesuitical.

Suits against Jones for threats and defamation are ongoing. A Wisconsin jury awarded one father of a boy killed at Sandy Hook $450,000 in a defamation case against a retired university professor who co-authored a book, *Nobody Died at Sandy Hook*.[63] In July 2021, Jones came out with a fresh charge: it was Hillary Clinton who organized the families suing him for defamation, and he "asked a Connecticut court to begin the process of issuing a subpoena to obtain records and testimony from the former secretary of state and Democratic presidential nominee.[64] But more and more suits have been successful. A Texas case in October 2021 was won by two Sandy Hook families, and in November a Connecticut Superior Court found Jones liable by default (he failed to produce documents). The jury's awards to eight families of victims are certain to bankrupt the conspiracist.[65]

From a societal standpoint, defamation law attempts to reconcile the value of avoiding media self-censorship with "our basic concept of the essential dignity and worth of every human being—a concept at the root of any decent system of ordered liberty."[66] We detect "the dignity and worth of every human being" when Veronique De La Rosa, the mother of Noah, explained why she is suing Jones: she wants to force him to admit "that Sandy Hook is real and that Noah was a real, living, breathing little boy who deserved to live out the rest of his life."[67]

Individual Harm and Civil Remedies: Intentional Infliction of Emotional Distress

Defamation is often combined with civil suits claiming intentional infliction of emotional distress (IIED). Ordinary meaning would tell us that conspiracist fabulations about the death of Seth Rich amounted to an intentional infliction of emotional distress on his family. Rich was a Democratic National Committee official murdered, police say, in a botched robbery. Seth's parents, Joel and Mary Rich, brought a suit against a Fox News reporter and a Fox contributor for public assertions that Seth was murdered because he leaked a trove of DNC emails to Wikileaks. Fox reported nonexistent findings of a "federal investigator" in an "FBI report," alleged confirming emails, aired fabricated quotes, and claimed "there's a lot out there."[68] The conspiracist story was designed to counter national intelligence agencies' judgment that the Russian government was behind the email dump and to absolve the Trump administration of Russian collusion. A week after airing several versions of the story, Fox removed it from its website, saying "it was not initially subjected to the high degree of editorial scrutiny we require for all our reporting ... upon appropriate review [it] was found not to meet those standards and has since been removed."[69]

Seth Rich's family persevered with their suit. IIED cases have turned on whether reporters' methods were "outrageous," so extreme as to be beyond the bounds of decency—violating privacy or pressure tactics or beleaguering grieving relatives.[70] The Riches were manipulated, lied to, and psychologically battered by reporters and the network. Yet District Court Judge George Daniels dismissed their case. On the merits, the emotional distress was real enough, the judge conceded, but the extremely high legal standard for IIED claims was not met. It requires not only intent to cause severe emotional distress, a causal connection between the conduct and the injury, and severe emotional distress, but also extreme and outrageous conduct.[71] It is not enough that the conduct of defendants is unprofessional, distasteful, or improper, or that it contains intentionally false statements or misrepresentations. Odiousness does not cross the line. To meet the standard, of extreme and outrageous conduct, the judge ruled, there must be a campaign of harassment or intimidation that is unrelenting, day in, day out, or be accompanied by physical threats.

Civil suits proceed one by one; they are expensive, and overall they are incommensurate with the dimension of conspiracist targeting of individuals. At the same time, for some they do hold out the possibility of vindication and compensation. And there is the possibility of broader containment of conspiracist attacks if the convoluted question of "public figure" is simplified, if recklessness is clarified, if what counts as a real-world threat in a universe of viral fabulations is reconsidered. These cases hold popular conspiracists to account, cause their videos and radio shows and postings to lose audience, and drive them into bankruptcy. That said, even winning suits are unlikely to deter the less prominent conspiracy entrepreneurs operating on innumerable dark sites, or ordinary men and women posting conspiracist charges, or the cruel or demented people provoked to harass and threaten their targets. The suits cannot reach anonymous propagators.

Two significant categorical exceptions to defamation law underscore its limitations in this age of rabid conspiracism. When high government officials are the source of conspiracist charges—the president and his political fellow travelers, the governor of Texas, elected Republican officials in Congress, and many others—there is no remedy apart from speaking truth to conspiracism. The Federal Tort Claims Act provides immunity for officials when it comes to slander, misrepresentation, and "deceit."[72] This exception has become more and more salient as conspiracism is increasingly initiated or assented to and spread by public officials. Still, there are good reasons not to remove immunity. It is not hard to imagine a chaos of nonstop litigation by political figures. And if courts were to take these cases on, it could "chill" the free-wheeling political speech—including hateful and noxious speech—that democracy requires. And nothing in exposing officials to defamation suits would extend to requiring truthfulness or civility overall.

There is a second, critical exception to defamation law as a recourse by private individuals: digital corporations are not subject to these suits. The 1996 Communications Decency Act protects them from liability for the bad acts of their users, and assumes that they are self-regulating "good Samaritans." The idea behind this exemption was that if the new internet technology was not granted broad immunity and if platforms were liable for content and consequences, they would not undertake responsible screening at all.[73] Do they?

Exit the Old Gatekeepers, Enter the New?

When publication was expensive, scholars, editors, and publishers decided what was worthy of dissemination. When the limited spectrum of public airways was the only way to broadcast voice and video, producers decided what was aired, the Fairness Doctrine mediated content, and public broadcasting was subsidized in the public interest. Conservatives railed against all these and advocated an unregulated market system for the media. They got their wish. There is no limit to the text and images that can be broadcast over Twitter, Facebook, YouTube, and websites like *Infowars,* and at virtually no cost. "More than 2.2 billion people, about a third of humanity, log in [to Facebook] at least once a month. . . . Facebook has as many adherents as Christianity."[74] Every day a billion things are posted there. These platforms enable individual expression capable of reaching a select audience of "friends" or masses of people and to do so anonymously. These platforms are "tailor-made for abuse by bad actors."[75]

Of course, we are our own censors and can choose to "block, mute, unfollow, log off, and even delete" their accounts.[76] But self-protection cannot disrupt digital threats to liberal democracy or harms to individuals unless people detach from these sites en masse—with negative consequences for free speech and associational pluralism of its own.

Gatekeeping happens, when it does, at the level of digital media corporations themselves. They are also self-regulating. These huge corporations have been called the "new sovereigns" with power to silence or to amplify voices. Alex Jones has no First Amendment right to post or tweet or host on privately owned platforms; he and his products can be removed item by item or banned outright. The global companies—Apple, Google, Facebook, YouTube, Twitter—have been slow to recognize their undefined "civic responsibility" and slow to reconceive themselves as public squares or public utilities subject to regulation. With the exception of policies already proscribed by law—bans on child pornography and removal of content to satisfy national laws (such as Nazi imagery in Germany) and bans on terrorist recruitment—they have no effective accountability for what they "publish" or what they censor. They have tiptoed into gatekeeping and, after the 2020 election and the January 6 insurrection, organized on their own websites as well as on others to take more aggressive action.

The internal forces operating against corporate gatekeeping are well known. These are profit-maximizing entities whose business is expanding the number of accounts—including "pages controlled by overseas 'troll factories'" and conspiracists bent on spewing false and inflammatory stories. The businesses mine users' data for advertising. In a phrase, it is a business model "driven by addiction and surveillance."[77] The precipitating events behind the demand for increased gatekeeping are also well known: revelations of Facebook's undisclosed use of personal information, third-party harvesting of private data, deliberate experiments with shaping users' behavior, platforms used as catalysts of violence in India and in Myanmar, the Russian interference operation in the US presidential election, and more. When the Trump campaign accepted Facebook's open offer to help political campaigns use their platform, Facebook employees helped craft messages hostile to ethnic minorities. The company could be directly blamed for fake news.[78]

Concern about popular conspiracists like Alex Jones also precipitated calls for corporate gatekeeping. When Sandy Hook parent Leonard Pozner published an open letter to Facebook's Mark Zuckerberg and described living in hiding because of death threats from conspiracists, Jones's sites were taken down. But response to dramatic individual appeals is not policy. In the summer of 2018, social media giants went further and removed conspiracist content produced by Jones and seemed to ban him from their platforms. Yet less than a month before Zuckerberg had condoned hosting pages dedicated to conspiracy theories like Jones's, insisting that "we don't take it down and ban people unless it's directly inciting violence."[79] There was no judgment that Jones was, in legal terms, inciting violence. What caused that change? It was Apple's decision to stop distributing Jones's podcasts as "hate speech" that led Facebook to act.[80] Apparently, the collective concern was reputational. The companies began to limit Jones's access to his huge audience. Still, it is unclear to what extent Jones was a special case owing to the spotlight on him. Or how many "strikes" he had against him to precipitate this action. It is not clear what limitations were actually imposed—initially not all his videos, podcasts, and posts were removed—or whether the restrictions are permanent.

Self-regulation is a moving target. A snapshot taken in February 2019 of corporate responses to Jones's conspiracist claims underscores the inconsistent and elusive character of gatekeeping.

- Justifying its decision, Facebook executives explained that Jones violated its community standards by "glorifying violence" and "using dehumanizing language to describe people who are transgender, Muslim, and immigrants."[81] The company did not reveal how it categorized Jones's specific individual violations or how many times his Facebook pages ran afoul of "community standards" before being removed. Facebook has experimented with "punishments" short of banning Jones: "reducing him" by using an algorithm that sent his messages to fewer people, suspending him for a month, and shutting down only specific pages. In January 2019, concerned with "recidivism," Facebook took down more pages linked to Jones.[82] In 2021 the company suspended Trump "indefinitely" for his "Big Lie" and for inciting violence.
- YouTube's "Community Guidelines" invite viewers to flag videos with nudity or sexual content or incitement to violence. Yet until it changed its content algorithms in 2019, YouTube's business model entailed recommending increasingly extremist videos to users.[83] Still, each "flagged" category is ambiguous. For example, YouTube hosts videos of the Islamic cleric whose sermons incited attackers in London though he did not directly call for violent jihad. Other violations count as child endangerment, including footage of a child being shoved to the ground. Jones's violations were videos said to amount to harassment and bullying against Parkland shooting survivor David Hogg.
- Apple is not a social media company; it offers apps, podcasts, songs, and videos—including neo-Nazi songs from iTunes. It has banned several *Infowars* podcasts for violating prohibitions against content that "could be construed as racist, misogynist, or homophobic" or that depict "graphic sex, violence, gore, illegal drugs, or hate themes." In addition, company policy justified removing the *Infowars* app (Apple's fourth most popular news app, "outranking every main-

stream news organization"), citing content that is "offensive, insensitive, upsetting, intended to disgust, or in exceptionally poor taste" or includes "realistic portrayals of people or animals being killed, maimed, tortured, or abused."[84]

- Twitter, the self-described "Free Speech Wing of the Free Speech Party," allows "potentially inflammatory" adult and violent content so long as it is not directed at an individual. Twitter banned Breitbart's Milo Yiannopolous in 2016 for "racist hate-trolling" against an actress.[85] But neither Jones's personal account nor his *Infowars* account were judged in violation of their policies: tweets claiming the Sandy Hook school shootings were staged remained on the site until August 2018, when Jones was temporarily suspended for posting a link to a video calling supporters to get their "battle rifles" ready for a fight against the press. Twitter CEO Jack Dorsey defended the position: "Accounts like Jones' can often sensationalize issues and spread unsubstantiated rumors, so it's critical journalists document, validate, and refute such information directly so people can form their own opinion. . . . This is what serves the public conversation best."[86] Nonetheless, Jones now seems to be banned from Twitter permanently for violating its "abusive behavior policy," which prohibits "excessively aggressive insults that target an individual, including content that contains slurs or similar language."[87] After the January 6 insurrection, Trump was permanently banned from twitter.

In sum, the editorial function at these sites is opaque and diffident; the standards are varied and vague.[88] Violent content is a particular problem—posts of murders, suicides, beheadings. Hate speech is a one-line rule among many other community standards and it is amorphous, indecipherable. And standards aside, gatekeeping is only as effective as its methods of enforcement, which are varied. Nonhuman algorithms flag content. Facebook employs 7,500 "moderators" worldwide to "sift through 10 million potentially rule-breaking posts per week," applying hundreds of rules developed to judge whether policies are violated.[89] Like other companies, it also relies on its billions of users to report "inappropriate content." The new corporate gatekeepers are stymied about both standards for censorship and how to organize enforcement—for good reason. As one CEO confessed, "We turned Alex Jones' Infowars away from our social platform but we're not sure why."[90]

Evan Osnos reflected on his interview with Facebook's Zuckerberg: "These are not technical puzzles to be cracked in the middle of the night but some of the subtlest aspects of human affairs, including the meaning of truth, the limits of free speech, and the origins of violence." He quotes historian Leslie Berlin: "The question Mark Zuckerberg is dealing with is: Should my company be the arbiter of truth and decency for two billion people?"[91]

Conspiracists and other bad actors banned from Facebook or Twitter migrate to other platforms—though they may lose visibility and followers. And other less conspicuous conspiracists continue to circulate and amplify the same stories. Text-based sites like Reddit and 4 chan seem to be more hands off.[92] A host of right-wing apps deliver curated messages, "free from the strictures and content guidelines imposed by Silicon Valley giants."[93] Complicating gatekeeping is the fact that conspiracism is also generated and spread anonymously, sites appear and disappear and appear again, and "recidivism" is common.

Officials and advocates of regulation circle around the question of government intervention into the self-regulating regime of the new media. They contemplate application of anti-trust law to challenge the concentration of power in the private hands of these huge corporations.[94] Or they discuss reforming Section 230 of the Communications Decency Act of 1996 to change the incentive of these corporations by exposing platforms to liability for acts by their users. The consequences of these proposals, enacted on a large scale, cannot be foreseen and worst-case scenarios are spun out: economic ruin (or further consolidation) of large corporations like Facebook or platforms self-protectively censoring all sorts of material. Proposals to prohibit techniques like anonymous bots and other forms of covert manipulation as strategies of containment are more compatible with free speech norms.

To date, the new gatekeepers' prescriptions have been negative: banning, changing algorisms to limit audiences, "demoting" conspiracist claims so that they are lower in newsfeeds, and so forth. But gatekeeping should not be a euphemism for private censorship *simpliciter*. If these platforms accept civic responsibility, there are other resources at their disposal besides censoring and demoting Jones. There are duties to warn. There are positive, educative measures such as promoting items that speak truth to conspiracy, providing steps by which users can rebuke and rebut conspiracism and other forms of disinformation.

An Old Question Raised Again

We are at a moment when the new conspiracism is paired with new technology, traditional gatekeepers have been displaced, technology eliminates barriers of cost and speed, and the architecture of communication is in the hands of all sorts of malignant actors. It is not just fringe quarters of the communication environment that can be described as a sewer of distortion, misinformation, disinformation, predation, vileness, and malice, and the new conspiracism is a critical part of this mix. It poses the unanticipated challenge of deeply illiberal assaults not only on foundational institutions of democratic public life but also on what it means to know something, epistemic polarization, and direct harm to individuals. The old question of free speech is raised again.

Pushback against censorship and containment derives from free speech principles embedded in law and political philosophy—principles grounded in a variety of liberal and democratic theories. Navigating the Scylla and Charybdis of unconstrained speech and regulated speech faces new rocks and shoals, and we need comprehensive accounts of how the new conspiracism and new technology change the argument. Up to now, discussions of containing conspiracism through private censorship or civil penalties have not been informed by theoretical discussion.[95] For up to now, the pros and cons of proposals to contain conspiracism are scattered in opinion pieces, essays in specialized journals dedicated to "communication" or technology, legal proposals for model regulations and legal briefs in some cases, and messaging from advocacy groups. The paramount concern about government regulation also applies to private corporate gatekeeping: Who guards the gatekeepers? Who should we trust? Who can protect public political life from degradation and individuals from direct personal harm? Partisanship often grounds these arguments: victims of conspiracism and progressive Democrats call for regulation, and Republicans attack Facebook for stifling conservative views.

I draw three broad conclusions from this exploration of the new conspiracism and its public and private harms. First, liberal democracy depends on pluralist sources of information and interpretation and opinion. The Millian argument, as well as directly democratic arguments for the conditions of collective deliberation and decision-making, are under a distinct kind of assault from conspiracism.

Yet, second, conspiracism's content is often a degraded form of political speech—content whose protection under the First Amendment law is firmly established. The prospect of government regulation or expanded legal liability raises the question of whether there exists what we can call a government "interest in truthful discourse." Is there a public corollary to a version of this buried in defamation law?[96] Changes in civil law can protect private individuals from harm. There may be particular venues in which fact-checking and other securities can be mandated and institutionalized. But protections for public life from degradation by conspiracism would require much more.

Third, runaway fabulist charges will be defanged, deterred, and contained not by regulatory law and public policy but popular resistance assisted by a responsible press and political representatives. Much of what can be done falls to citizens themselves. It requires the obvious: general openness to knowledge and guarded skepticism and bringing both to bear in a degraded environment.[97] It requires digital platforms to make reporting and correction accessible. Perhaps it requires rewards for support of informal norms of civility and social disapproval for violations. The new conspiracism is not the only force producing disorientation, provoking outrage at damaging public life with impunity, and tempting us to give over protection and correction to official guardians. But conspiracy without the theory is a new, unanticipated, and now very clear case of public and private harm. It continues to shape public and private life. Its dangerous assault on democratic institutions and common sense is not about to retreat to the fringes.

Notes

1. Cited in Aaron Cooper, "Six More Sandy Hook families Sue Broadcaster Alex Jones," CNN, August 6, 2018, https://www.cnn.com/2018/05/23/us/alex-jones-sandy-hook-suit.

2. Cited in defendants' motion to dismiss in *Pozner and De La Rosa v. Alex Jones*, District Court of Travis Texas, no. D-1-GN-18–001842

3. Russell Muirhead and Nancy L. Rosenblum, *A Lot of People Are Saying: The New Conspiracism and the Assault on Democracy* (Princeton, NJ: Princeton University Press, 2019).

4. Elizabeth Williamson, "Truth in a Post-Truth Era: Sandy Hook Families Sue Alex Jones, Conspiracy Theorist," *New York Times*, May 23, 2018, https://www.nytimes.com/2018/05/23/us/politics/alex-jones-trump-sandy-hook.html.

5. Faiz Siddiqui and Susan Svrluga, "N.C. Man Told Police He Went to D.C. Pizzeria with Gun to Investigate Conspiracy Theory," *Washington Post*, December 5, 2016, https://www.washingtonpost.com/news/local/wp/2016/12/04/d-c-police-respond-to-report-of-a-man-with-a-gun-at-comet-ping-pong-restaurant/?utm_term=.0ffba0f83aec. On Russian contributions to the Pizzagate narrative, see Timothy Snyder, *The Road to Unfreedom* (New York: Tim Duggan Books, 2018), 246. Pizzagate was the progenitor of QAnon. Rosenblum was a contributor to PBS's *Frontline* documentary "The United States of Conspiracy," aired July 2020: https://www.pbs.org/wgbh/frontline/interview/nancy-rosenblum/.

6. David Montero, "Alex Jones Settles Chobani Lawsuit and Retracts Comments about Refugees in Twin Falls, Idaho," *Los Angeles Times*, May 17, 2017, http://www.latimes.com/nation/la-na-chobani-alex-jones-20170517-story.html; Mallory Shelbourne, "Infowars' Alex Jones Apologizes for Pushing 'Pizzagate' Conspiracy Theory," *The Hill*, March 25, 2017, https://thehill.com/homenews/325761-infowars-alex-jones-apologizes-for-pushing-pizzagate-conspiracy-theory.

7. Williamson, "Truth in a Post-Truth Era."

8. Stephanie K. Baer, "An Armed Man Spouting a Bizarre Right-Wing Conspiracy Theory Was Arrested after a Standoff at the Hoover Dam," *Buzzfeed*, June 17, 2018, https://www.buzzfeednews.com/article/skbaer/qanon-believer-arrested-hoover-dam.

9. Elizabeth Williamson and Emily Steel, "Conspiracy Theories Made Alex Jones Very Rich. They May Bring Him Down," *New York Times*, September 7, 2018, https://www.nytimes.com/2018/09/07/us/politics/alex-jones-business-infowars-conspiracy.html.

10. The picture is of gender disparity. QAnon welcomes (anonymous) contributors but advises women to conceal their gender and to merge into the aggressive male culture of the sites. McKew argues that the anti-woman animus began in 2014–15 with Gamergate, when women gamers objected to the misogyny of the videogaming culture. Molly McKew, "Brett Kavanaugh and the Information Terrorists Trying to Reshape America," *Wired*, October 3, 2018, https://www.wired.com/story/information-terrorists-trying-to-reshape-america/.

11. Williamson, "Truth in a Post-Truth Era."

12. Williamson and Steel, "Conspiracy Theories."

13. Cited in Matt Ford, "The Legal War on Alex Jones," *New Republic*, May 29, 2018, https://newrepublic.com/article/148562/legal-war-on-alex-jones.

14. Williamson and Steel, "Conspiracy Theories."

15. Williamson, "Truth in a Post-Truth Era."

16. Williamson and Steel, "Conspiracy Theories."

17. Evan Osnos, "Ghost in the Machine: Can Mark Zuckerberg Fix Facebook before It Breaks Democracy?," *New Yorker*, September 17, 2018, 32–47, at 47.

18. Kate Starbird, "Information Wars: A Window into the Alternative Media Ecosystem," https://medium.com/hci-design-at-uw/information-wars-a-window-into-the-alternative-media-ecosystem-a1347f32fd8f.

19. Eli Rosenberg, "Alex Jones Apologizes for Promoting 'Pizzagate' Hoax," *New York Times*, March 25, 2017, https://www.nytimes.com/2017/03/25/business/alex-jones-pizzagate-apology-comet-ping-pong.html.

20. Starbird, "Information Wars."

21. Bernard Bailyn, *The Ideological Origins of the American Revolution* (Cambridge, MA: Harvard University Press, 1967), 95.

22. Bruno Latour speaks of "those mad mixtures of knee-jerk disbelief, punctilious demands for proofs, and free use of powerful explanation from the social neverland" in *Politics of Nature: How to Bring the Sciences into Democracy* (Cambridge, MA: Harvard University Press, 2004), 230.

23. David Wiegel, "What the Media Gets Wrong about Donald Trump's Obama-Muslim Flap," *Washington Post*, September 18, 2015, https://www.washingtonpost.com/news/the-fix/wp/2015/09/18/why-nobody-can-agree-on-what-donald-trump-said-about-muslims/?utm_term=.875f4796fef9.

24. Some philosophers would argue that all beliefs rest on a kind of true-enoughness, or verisimilitude. On this view, we never validate our beliefs to the point of perfect certainty; we can only attempt to falsify them, and beliefs that have stood the test of falsification are corroborated. True-enoughness, by contrast, is not subject to any falsification test. If it seems possible, it satisfies the true-enough test.

25. Daniel A. Effron, "Why Trump Supporters Don't Mind His Lies," *New York Times*, April 28, 2018, https://www.nytimes.com/2018/04/28/opinion/sunday/why-trump-supporters-dont-mind-his-lies.html.

26. Sheryl Estrada, "Completely Plausible says Republican Lawmaker," *Diversity Inc*, August 22, 2017, https://www.diversityinc.com/news/completely-plausible-obama-staged-charlottesville-events-smear-trump-says-republican-lawmaker.

27. MorningConsult/Politico poll, cited in Steven Levitsky and Daniel Ziblatt, *How Democracies Die* (New York: Crown, 2018), 197.

28. Ipsos/Reuters poll, The Big Lie, https://www.ipsos.com/sites/default/files/ct/news/documents/2021-05/Ipsos%20Reuters%20Topline%20Write%20up-%20The%20Big%20Lie%20-%2017%20May%20thru%2019%20May%202021.pdf.

29. Richard Hofstadter, *The Paranoid Style in American Politics and Other Essays* (Cambridge, MA: Harvard University Press, 1964), 31.

30. For example, the rumor that as a result of the Trump administration's "zero-tolerance" policy and the forcible separation of migrant children from their families, the government had "lost" 1,500 children. The data came from 2014 under different circumstances; though the claim was repeated widely it was quickly corrected and those who had repeated it, like Senator Ed Markey from Massachusetts, retracted the charge. https://www.cnn.com/2018/05/29/us/immigration-refugee-child-missing-hhs-obama-photo-trnd/index.html.

31. Brendan Nyhan, "Why the 'Death Panel' Myth Wouldn't Die: Misinformation in the Health Care Reform Debate," *The Forum* 8, no. 1, (2010).

32. Aaron Blake, "Infowars is Behind President Trump's Idea that the Media is Covering Up Terrorist Attacks," *Washington Post*, February 6, 2017, https://www.washingtonpost.com/news/the-fix/wp/2017/02/06/trumps-suggestion-that-the-media-is-ignoring-terrorist-attacks-has-a-familiar-source-infowars/.

33. Charles Sykes, "Why Nobody Cares the President Is Lying," *New York Times*, February 4, 2017. https://www.nytimes.com/2017/02/04/opinion/sunday/why-nobody-cares-the-president-is-lying.html.

34. Jodi Dean, "Theorizing Conspiracy Theory," *Theory and Event*, 4, no. 3 (2000): 2, 6; at https://muse.jhu.edu/article/32599.

35. Kate Starbird, "Information Wars"; Danah Boyd, "You Think You Want Media Literacy.... Do You?," originally delivered March 2018, South by Southwest keynote, Austin, TX, "What Hath We Wrought?," https://points.datasociety.net/you-think-you-want-media-literacy-do-you-7cad6af18ec2.

36. District Court of Travis County, Texas, 345th District Court, Cause no. D-1-GN-18-001842. Also quoted in Williamson, "Truth in a Post-Truth Era." One of the parents in the lawsuit, Wheeler, was once an actor.

37. Williamson and Steel, "Conspiracy Theories."

38. David Atkins, "The Q-Anon Conspiracy Is Still Destroying Lives and Families," *Washington Monthly*, December 9, 2018, https://washingtonmonthly.com/2018/12/09/the-q-anon-conspiracy-theory-is-still-destroying-lives-and-families.

39. Cited in defendants' motion to dismiss in *Pozner and De La Rosa v. Alex Jones, District Court of Travis Texas*, no. D-1-GN-18-001842.

40. The phrase is from Robert Jay Lifton, *The Climate Swerve* (New York: New Press, 2017), 93. For a full discussion see Nancy L. Rosenblum, "Witnessing Climate Change," *Daedalus* 149, no. 4 (Fall 2020).

41. Yochai Benkler, Robert Faris, and Hal Roberts, "Epistemic Crisis," Oxford Scholarship Online, 357, http://www.oxfordscholarship.com/view/10.1093/oso/9780190923624.001.0001/oso-9780190923624-chapter-1.

42. Brendan Nyhan, "Why the Fact-Checking at Facebook Needs to be Checked," *New York Times*, October 23, 2017, https://www.nytimes.com/2017/10/23/upshot/why-the-fact-checking-at-facebook-needs-to-be-checked.html. For an overview, see Chloe Wittenberg and Adam J. Berinsky, "Misinformation and Its Correction," unpublished paper on file with the author.

43. Heather Digby Parton, "Right-wing Lunatics Think the Military Is Planning to Invade Texas: Here's Why," *Salon.com*, April 30, 2015, https://www.salon.com/2015/04/30/right_wing_lunatics_think_the_military_is_planning_to_invade_texas_heres_why/.

The New Conspiracism: Public and Private Harm and Immunity from the Law **129**

44. Patrick Svitek, "Abbott's Letter Elevates Jade Helm 15 Concerns," *Texas Tribune*, April 30, 2015, http://www.texastribune.org/2015/04/30/abbotts-letter-puts-jade-helm-national-stage/.

45. Sunstein and Vermeuele, "Conspiracy Theories: Cause and Effect," *Journal of Political Philosophy* 17, no. 2 (2009): 202–227 at 219; 221.

46. "Intelligence Activities and the Rights of Americans, Book II, Final Report of the Select Committee to Study Governmental Operations with Respect to Intelligence Activities," US Senate, April 26, 1976, see "3. Covert Action and the Use of Illegal or Improper Means," https://www.intelligence.senate.gov/sites/default/files/94755_II.pdf.

47. Sam Leith, "Nothing Like the Truth," *Times Literary Supplement*, August 16, 2017, https://www.the-tls.co.uk/articles/public/post-truth-sam-leith/.

48. *Gertz v. Robert Welch, Inc.*, 418 U.S. 323 (1974) at 349.

49. Rob Ryser, "Why Alex Jones wants US Supreme Court to rule on his 'blood on the streets rant,'" https://www.newstimes.com/local/article/Supreme-Court-upholds-sanctions-for-Alex-Jones-15429879.php.

50. Plaintiffs' Original Petition and Request for Disclosure at 15, *Pozner and De La Rosa v. Alex Jones, District Court of Travis Texas*, No. D-1-GN-18–001842 (Dist. Ct. of Travis Co., Tex., April 16, 2018).

51. Williamson and Steel, "Conspiracy Theories."

52. Matt Ford, "The Legal War on Alex Jones," *New Republic*, May 29, 2018, https://newrepublic.com/article/148562/legal-war-on-alex-jones.

53. David Montero, "Alex Jones Settles Chobani Lawsuit."

54. More specifically, the real purpose of the suit is to make new state law that "opens Texas' citizens to civil liability should they openly question the government and/or craft any type of 'conspiracy theory' or differing view to that which is reported by the mainstream media." Defendants' Motion to Dismiss under the Texas Citizens' Participation Act at 3, *Pozner and De La Rosa v. Alex Jones, District Court of Travis Texas*, No. D-1-GN-18–001842 (Dist. Ct. of Travis Co., Tex., April 16, 2018).

55. Timothy Burke, "Alex Jones Is Still Talking about a Sandy Hook Conspiracy Theory," *Daily Beast*, February 25, 2019, https://www.thedailybeast.com/alex-jones-is-still-talking-about-the-sandy-hook-conspiracy-theory.

56. Williamson, "Alex Jones of Infowars Destroyed Evidence Related to Sandy Hook Suits, Motion Says," *New York Times*, August 17, 2018, https://www.nytimes.com/2018/08/17/us/politics/alex-jones-evidence-infowars.html.

57. *Gertz v. Robert Welch, Inc.* at 345–346.

58. Emma Grey Ellis, "Win or Lose, the Alex Jones Lawsuit Will Help Redefine Free Speech," *Wired*, August 6, 2018, https://www.wired.com/story/alex-jones-lawsuit-will-help-redefine-free-speech/.

59. Ellis, "Win or Lose."

60. Defendants' Motion to Dismiss Under the Texas Citizens' Participation Act at 37, *Pozner and De La Rosa v. Alex Jones, District Court of Travis Texas*, No. D-1-GN-18–001842 (Dist. Ct. of Travis Co., Tex., April 16, 2018). Emphasis added by the defendant.

61. Allan Smith, "'It's Performance Art': Lawyer for Alex Jones says InfoWars founder is 'playing a character,'" *Business Insider*, April 17, 2017, https://www.businessinsider.com/lawyer-alex-jones-infowars-playing-character-acting-2017-4.

62. River Clegg, "New Social-Media Users Guide," *New Yorker*, October 15, 2018, https://www.newyorker.com/magazine/2018/10/15/new-social-media-user-guidelines.

63. Louis Casiano, "Sandy Hook father awarded $450,000 in defamation suit against university professor," *Fox News*, October 16, 2019, https://www.foxnews.com/us/sandy-hook-father-awarded-450000-in-defamation-suit-against-university-professor.

64. Sebastian Murdock, "Alex Jones Asks Court to Make Hillary Clinton Testify in Sandy Hook Defamation Case," *Huffington Post*, July 2, 2021, https://www.huffpost.com/entry/alex-jones-subpoenas-hillary-clinton-to-testify-in-sandy-hook-defamation-case_n_60df274fe4b0ad1785db454a.

65. "Sandy Hook: Alex Jones Liable in Defamation Lawsuit," BBC, https://www.bbc.com/news/world-us-canada-59298320.

66. Justice Stewart in *Curtis Publishing*, cited in *Gertz* at 481 US 341.

67. Williamson, "Truth in a Post-Truth Era."

68. Meagan Flynn, "Fox News Sued by Parents of Seth Rich, Slain DNC Staffer, over Conspiracy Theory about His Death," *Washington Post*, March 14, 2018, https://www.washingtonpost.com/news/morning-mix/wp/2018/03/14/fox-news-sued-by-parents-of-seth-rich-slain-dnc-staffer-for-conspiracy-theory-about-his-death/.

69. Mike Snider, "Judge Dismisses Case against Fox News by Parents of Slain DNC Staffer Seth Rich," *USA Today*, August 3, 2018, https://www.usatoday.com/stor/money/media/2018/08/03/seth-rich-slaying-judge-dismisses-parents-case-against-fox-news/900313002/.

70. Karen Markin, "The Truth Hurts: Intentional Infliction of Emotional Distress as a Cause of Action against the Media," *Communication Law and Policy* 5, no. 4 (2000): 469–503.

71. All quotes are from *Rich v Fox News Network, LLC, Malia Zimmerman, and Ed Butowsky*, George Daniels, US District Judge, Memorandum Decision and Order. 18 Civ. 2223 (GBD), filed August 2, 2018.

72. Aziz Huq, "When Government Defames," *New York Times*, August 10, 2017, https://www.nytimes.com/2017/08/10/opinion/government-defamation-white-house-slander.html .

73. DaNielle Keats Citron and Benjamin Wittes, *The Internet Will Not Break: Denying Bad Samaritans @230 Immunity*, 86 Fordham Law Review 401 (2017).

74. Osnos, "Ghost in the Machine," 34, 46.

75. Roger McNamee, cited in Jacob Weisberg, "The Autocracy APP," *New York Review of Books*, October 25, 2018, 20–22, at 20.

76. Peter Suderman, "The Slippery Slope of Regulating Social Media," *New York Times*, September 11, 2018, https://www.nytimes.com/2018/09/11/opinion/the-slippery-slope-of-regulating-social-media.html.

77. Weisberg, "The Autocracy APP," 20.

78. Osnos, "Ghost in the Machine," 42.

79. Osnos, "Ghost in the Machine," 46.

80. Sheera Frenkel, Daisuke Wakabayashi, Kate Conger, and Jack Nicas, "Gatekeepers or Censors? How Tech Manages Online Speech," *New York Times*, August 7, 2018, https://www.nytimes.com/2018/08/07/technology/tech-companies-online-speech.html. My summaries here cite this piece.

81. Facebook Newsroom, "Enforcing Our Community Standards," https://newsroom.fb.com/news/2018/08/enforcing-our-community-standards/.

82. Christina Zhao, "Facebook Removes Over 20 Pages Linked to Conspiracy Theorist Alex Jones, Infowars," https://www.newsweek.com/facebook-removes-over-20-pages-linked-conspiracy-theorist-alex-jones-infowars-1319518.

83. Fruzsina Eordogh, "YouTube Stops Recommending Conspiracy Videos, Finally," *Forbes*, January 28, 2019, https://www.forbes.com/sites/fruzsinaeordogh/2019/01/28/youtube-stops-recommending-conspiracy-videos-finally/?sh=17e862ed77cf.

84. Frenkel et al., "Gatekeepers or Censors?"; Williamson and Steel, "Conspiracy Theories."
85. McKew, "Brett Kavanaugh."
86. https://twitter.com/jack/status/1026984249960755200?lang=en.
87. Issie Lapowsky, "Twitter Finally Axes Alex Jones—Over a Publicity Stunt," *Wired*, September 6, 2018, https://www.wired.com/story/twitter-bans-alex-jones-infowars/. On the earlier temporary suspension, see Williamson, "Alex Jones of Infowars Destroyed Evidence."
88. One proposal for simplification is to apply the standards of defamation law: David French, "A Better Way to Ban Alex Jones," *New York Times*, August 7, 2018, https://www.nytimes.com/2018/08/07/opinion/alex-jones-infowars-facebook.html.
89. Sandra E. Garcia, "Ex-Content Moderator Sues Facebook, Saying Violent Images Caused her PTSD," *New York Times*, September 25, 2018, https://www.google.com/search?client=safari&rls=en&q=Ex-Content+Moderator+Sues+Facebook%2C+saying+Saying+Violent+Images+Caused+her+PTSD&ie=UTF-8&oe=UTF-8.
90. Benjamin Vaughan, "We Turned Alex Jones' Infowars Away from Our Social Platform but We're Not Sure Why," *Forbes*, January 29, 2019, https://www.forbes.com/sites/benjaminvaughan/2019/01/29/we-turned-alex-jones-infowars-away-from-our-social-platform-but-were-not-sure-why/?sh=335ada326411.
91. Osnos, "Ghost in the Machine," 35.
92. Caitlin Carlson, "Censoring Hate Speech in the U.S. Social Media Content: Understanding the User's Perspective," *Communications Law Review* 17, no. 1: 24–45 at 31.
93. Natasha Singer and Nicholas Confessore, "Republicans Find a Facebook Work-around: Their Own Apps," *New York Times*, October 20, 2018, https://www.nytimes.com/2018/10/20/technology/politics-apps-conservative-republican.html.
94. Danielle Citron and Quita Jurecic, "Platform Justice: Content Moderation at an Inflection Point," *Lawfare*, September 7, 2018, https://www.lawfareblog.com/platform-justice-content-moderation-inflection-point (referring to the 2018 Fighting Online Sex Trafficking act [FOST] and amending the Communications Decency Act).
95. For a probing piece, see Joshua Cohen and Archon Fung, "Democracy and the Digital Public Sphere," Digital Technology and Democratic Theory Workshop, June 2018, paper on file with the author.
96. *U.S. v. Alvarez*, 567 US 709.
97. A growing literature on digital literacy includes Sam Wineburg, Sarah McGrew, Jol Breakstone, and Teresa Ortega, "Evaluating Information: The Cornerstone of Civic Online Reasoning," Stanford Digital Repository, available at http://purl.stanford.edu/fv751yt5934.

Contributors

ELIZABETH S. ANKER, Department of English, Cornell University

LAWRENCE DOUGLAS, Department of Law, Jurisprudence and Social Thought, Amherst College

JEREMY KESSLER, School of Law, Columbia University

Sharon R. Krause, Department of Political Science, Brown University

LEE MCINTYRE, Center for Philosophy and History of Science, Boston University

NANCY L. ROSENBLUM, Department of Government, Harvard University

AUSTIN SARAT, Departments of Law, Jurisprudence and Social Thought and Political Science, Amherst College

MARTHA MERRELL UMPHREY, Department of Law, Jurisprudence and Social Thought, Amherst College

Index

Abbott, Greg, 113
abuse of power: as fostered by neoliberalism, 16–24; Locke on arbitrary power, 24–28; Mill on social power, 30–31; Montesquieu on self-limiting institutional framework, 28–30; restraining, via classical liberalism, 31–38
Acosta, Jim, 83
Adams, John, 88
administrative government and illiberalism, 62–77; administrative government, defined, 63; congressional delegation to administrative government, 66–68, 70; historical function of administrative law, 65–66; illiberal democracy (populism) vs. undemocratic liberalism (technocracy), 62, 72–73; internal administrative law, as liberal check, 67–68; internal administrative law, growth of, 68–70; judicial supervision of administrative government, 11, 64, 67, 70, 71; liberal democratic crisis and, 62–64; "presidentialism" and, 11, 66, 70–72; procedural protection of regulated private parties, 66–70
Albright, Madeleine, 81–82, 93–94
Alefantis, James, 104
Alito, Samuel, 5
All That Is Solid Melts into Air (Berman), 46–49

Amnesty International, 54
"Anti-Fascist" rallies (August 2017), 94
anti-liberalism of neoliberalism. *See* neoliberalism as anti-liberalism
Apple, 121–23
Arendt, Hannah, 80, 99n21
The Assault on Intelligence (Hayden), 82
authoritarianism. *See* post-truth and authoritarianism

backfire effect, 112
Bailyn, Bernard, 106
Balibar, Etienne, 55
Bannon, Steve, 64
Barr, William "Bill," 8
Baudelaire, Charles, 47
Berlin, Isaiah, 1
Berlin, Leslie, 124
Berman, Marshall, 46–49, 74nn1–2
Bernstein, Richard, 88–89
Biden, Joe, 9, 95–96
Biden Center (University of Pennsylvania), 98n9
Bigsby, Christopher, 78
"birtherism," 109
The Body in Pain (Scarry), 53–54
Bolsonaro, Jair, 3, 7
Brazil, rise of illiberalism in, 3, 7
Britain: limitation of political power and, 28; post-truth in, 78–79
Brookings Institution, 81
Brown, Wendy, 16, 18, 23, 34, 35–36, 44
Burns, Jennifer, 38–39n4

135

Bush, George H. W., 6
Butler, Judith, 49, 51–52

campaign finance, corporate money in, 32
Charles IX (king of France), 29
Charlottesville protest (2017), 107
Cheney, Liz, 96
Chevron, 22
Chicago School. *See* Friedman, Milton
Chile, human rights in, 34–35
Chobani, 115
Citizens United (2010), 35, 44
civil resistance: civil remedies in response to new conspiracism, 114–20; to post-truth, 92–95; speaking truth to conspiracy, 111–14. *See also* individuals
class: administrative government and New Deal, 71–72; Marxist thought on classical liberalism, 3–4
class-action lawsuits, 32–33
classical liberalism: free speech and, 45; as restraint on neoliberalism, 9–10, 24–31, 35; speaking truth to controversy as, 103
Clinton, Hillary, 103, 105, 111, 118
CNN: Gergen on fake news, 80–81; Trump's accusation of fake news against, 83
Cold War censorship, 53–57
Coles, Rom, 35
Comet Ping Pong, 104
Communications Decency Act (1996), 120, 124
Congress. *See* United States Congress
conspiracy theory vs. new conspiracism, 106. *See also* new conspiracism
Contingency, Irony, Solidarity (Rorty), 47–48
continued influence effect, 112
corporate power: campaign finance and, 32; *Citizens United*, 35, 44; confinement and exploitation of consumers, 22–25, 30–37; consumer sovereignty and, 21–22; corporate speech as uncensorable, 44, 45, 59; digital media corporations as gatekeepers, 120–24; of monopolies, 21, 40n27; worker exploitation and, 3–4. *See also individual names of corporations*
courts: administrative agencies at cross-purposes and, 11; judicial supervision of administrative government, 11, 64, 67, 70, 71; Supreme Court on "Muslim travel ban," 8; Supreme Court on pornography, 4; Trump's lawsuits about 2020 election, 101n57
Cover, Robert, 52, 61n23
Crenshaw, Kimberle, 50, 61n17
"crisis actors," 103. *See also* new conspiracism
Critical Inquiry, "Has Critique Run out of Steam?" (Latour), 57–58
critical race theory (CRT). *See* race
critical theory and free speech, 44–50
Cruz, Ted, 105, 107

Daniels, George, 119
Dawes, Simon, 39n4
The Death of Democracy (Hett), 90
defamation, 114–20. *See also* new conspiracism
De La Rosa, Veronique, 118
de Man, Paul, 49
democracy: administrative government and tension with, 62–64, 73; Rousseau on "preexistence of a People," 55; rule of law as principle of, 88; threats of new conspiracism to, 102–3, 108. *See also* administrative government and illiberalism; elections and voting; free speech; law and illiberalism; neoliberalism as anti-liberalism; new conspiracism; post-truth and authoritarianism
The Democratic Paradox (Mouffe), 56
Department of Justice, 8

Derrida, Jacques, 49, 58
Dewey, John, 19
Dionne, E. J., 81
Di Paola, Marcelo, 23
discourse. *See* free speech
disinformation vs. misinformation, 84–86. *See also* new conspiracism; post-truth and authoritarianism
Dorsey, Jack, 123
"double delegation," 73, 77n39
Du Bois, W. E. B., 51
Duda, Andrzej, 3, 7

economic power: abuse of, 17–24; classical liberalism for restraint on, 31–35, 37; Friedman on political power joined with, 42n82; Hayek on human knowledge of economic systems, 19–20; marketplace of ideas, 30; Mill on, 30–31; Montesquieu on, 28–30; physical coercion by economic agents, 21–24; property rights, 26–28; self-regulating markets, 39n13
elections and voting: conspiracism and extremism in Republican Party, 112–13; electoral dictatorship, 89–90, 100n43; encouraging democratic process for, 93–94; "In a New Poll, Half of Republicans Say They Would Support Postponing the 2020 Election if Trump Proposed It," 100n45; January 6 insurrection, 95–97, 115, 123; Republican Party and 2020 presidential election, 95, 96; Special Counsel's Investigation (2016 election), 86–89; Trump's lawsuits about 2020 election, 101n57; voter suppression laws in United States, 96. *See also* post-truth and authoritarianism
epistemic polarization, 103, 109–11
Erdogan, Recep, 3, 7, 89–90
executive branch (United States): Congress polarized from, 64; free speech manipulated by, 8–9;

"presidentialism," 11, 66, 70–72, 76n21. *See also individual names of presidents*
extractive zones, 40n38

Facebook: new conspiracism and, 13, 105, 112, 120–24; post-truth and authoritarianism and, 31; social power of, 31
fact-checking. *See* post-truth and authoritarianism
Fairness Doctrine, 120
fake news, 79, 97–98n4, 98n19, 99n20, 109–11. *See also* new conspiracism; post-truth and authoritarianism
Falwell, Jerry, 117
fascism. *See* post-truth and authoritarianism
Fascism (Albright), 81–82
Federal Tort Claims Act (1946), 119–20
Fidesz (Hungarian political party), 8
First Amendment. *See* freedom of the press; free speech
Fisher v. University of Texas (2016), 5
Foreign Affairs, "The Rise of Illiberal Democracy" (Zakaria), 3
Foucault, Michel, 22, 49, 51, 58
Fox News, and new conspiracism, 103, 118
France, and limitation of political power, 28, 29
freedom of the press: fake news as threat to, 82–86; supporting, 93
free speech, 43–61; authoritarianism as consequence of, 58–60; Cold War censorship and radical democracy, 53–57; irony of left-leaning radicalism, 46–50; legal system and censorship enforcement, 50–53; liberal legality of, 4–5; neoliberalism and, 34, 35; neoliberalism, anti-liberalism, and illiberalism distinctions, 44–46; new conspiracism and, 103, 116, 120, 123–26;

free speech (*continued*)
  pornography as, 4; right-leaning weaponization of free speech, 7–9, 43–44, 57–58. *See also* new conspiracism; post-truth and authoritarianism
Friedman, Milton: on economic joined with political power, 42n82; on liberalism as "laissez faire at home," 39n6; neoliberalism as anti-liberalism and, 18, 20, 21, 26, 31, 34–35, 37; S. Jones on, 40n27, 40n29

Gamergate, 127n10
gatekeepers, digital media corporations as, 120–24
Gates, Henry Louis, 51
gender: free speech used for male domination, 4; "men's rights" movement, 59; QAnon and gender disparity, 127n10; women of color excluded by legal system, 50–52, 61n17
Gender Trouble (Butler), 51–52
George W. Bush Institute, 98n9
Gergen, David, 80–81
Gertz v. Robert Welch Inc. (1974), 116
Gessen, Masha, 80
Gibson-Graham, J. K., 33
Goebbels, Josef, 94–95
Gomez-Barris, Macarena, 40n38
Google, 31
Gordon, Jill, 42n77
government. *See* state power
Gowder, Paul, 92

Harvey, David, 22–23, 38n4
"Has Critique Run out of Steam?" (Latour), 57–58
Hawley, Josh, 107
Hayden, Michael V., 82
Hayek, F. A., 19–20, 26, 31, 34–35, 39n6, 40n29, 42n96
Heidegger, Martin, 6
Hett, Benjamin Carter, 90
Hitler, Adolf, 80

Hobhouse, L. T., 19
Hofstadter, Richard, 108
Hogg, David, 122
Hoover, J. Edgar, 113
How Democracies Die (Levitsky & Ziblatt), 96–97
How Propaganda Works (Stanley), 79
Huguenots, Bayonne massacre plan, 29
Hungary, rise of illiberalism in, 3, 7, 8
Huq, Aziz, 90
Hustler magazine, defamation lawsuit, 117

illiberal democracy. *See* populism vs. technocracy
"The Illuminations of Hannah Arendt" (Bernstein), 88–89
illusory truth effect (repetition effect), 87, 94–95
"In a New Poll, Half of Republicans Say They Would Support Postponing the 2020 Election if Trump Proposed It" (Malka & Lelkes), 100n45
individuals: civil resistance by, 92–95, 114–20; harm to, from new conspiracism, 103, 114–20; individual agency eroded by neoliberalism, 22–25, 30–37; state power required for liberty of, 1–3; violence in "extractive zones," 40n38
Infowars (Jones). *See* Jones, Alex
Instagram, 31
intelligence community: calls for infiltration of conspiracist groups, 113–14; on fake news, 82
intentional infliction of emotional distress (IIED), 118–20. *See also* new conspiracism
intersectionality theory, 50
irony of radical left, 46–50
"It Can Happen Here" (Sunstein), 93

Jade Helm 15, 113
Jamieson, Dale, 23
January 6 insurrection, 95–97, 115, 123

Index

Jones, Alex, 102–5, 110, 111, 113–18, 121–23
Jones, Stedman, 39n4, 40n27, 40n29
journalism. *See* freedom of the press

Kagan, Elena, 43
Kant, Immanuel, 1
Kavanaugh, Brett, 103
Kennedy, Duncan, 57
Koch brothers, 30

labor and neoliberalism, 32–35
Lacan, Jacques, 51, 55, 58
"laissez faire," liberalism as, 39n6
language: power as totalitarian relationship to, 54–55; as symbolic, 48; violence perpetrated by, 49
Lanza, Adam, 115
Latour, Bruno, 43, 57–58, 127n22
law and illiberalism, 1–15; illiberalism, defined, 3; illiberalism of free speech, 4–5, 7–9; law and liberalism relationship, 1–3; Marxist thought on classical liberalism and, 3–4; sovereign decisionism and, 6–7. *See also* administrative government and illiberalism; free speech; neoliberalism as anti-liberalism; new conspiracism; post-truth and authoritarianism
Law's Abnegation (Vermeule), 65–66
Lefort, Claude, 55
Lelkes, Yphtach, 100n45
Levitsky, Steven, 96–97
Lewis, Sinclair, 81
liberalism: administrative government as threat to, 62–64, 66, 76n20; freedom of press/rule of law as values of, 82–89; as "laissez faire," 39n6; populism vs. technocracy and, 62, 72–73, 74n1; state power required for individuals' rights, 1–3
Locke, John: modern-day neoliberalism and, 17, 19, 38, 41n56; on personal liberty and state rights, 1, 2; *Second Treatise of Government*, 24–28, 30

Lorde, Audre, 49
A Lot of People Are Saying (Muirhead & Rosenblum), 102
lying. *See* post-truth and authoritarianism

MacKinnon, Catharine, 4
Madison, James, 1
Malka, Ariel, 100n45
Manne, Kate, 43
"March for Science" (April 2017), 94
marketplace of ideas, 30
Markey, Ed, 128n30
Marx, Karl, and Marxism, 3–4, 47
Matsuda, Mari, 51
Mayer, Milton, 90, 93
McCann, Sean, 48
McIntyre, Lee, 83
McKew, Molly, 127n10
"men's rights" movement, 59
Metzger, Gillian, 68
Mill, J. S.: on individual liberty vs. state power, 1, 2, 8, 9; neoliberalism and, 17, 19, 22, 30–31, 38; *On Liberty*, 30–31, 42n77; *Principles of Political Economy*, 41–42n76
Mirowski, Philip, 40n27
Mises, Ludwig von, 21–22, 26
misinformation vs. disinformation, 84–86. *See also* new conspiracism; post-truth and authoritarianism
Montesquieu, Baron de, 1, 9, 17, 19, 28–30, 32, 38
Mouffe, Chantal, 56
Mounk, Yascha, 100n43
Mueller, Robert, 86–88
Muirhead, Russell, 102
"Muslim travel ban," 8
Myanmar, military coup (2021), 96–97

Nader, Ralph, 45
National Security Agency, 82
Nazis and Third Reich: authoritarianism of, 80; citizens' role in, 90; propaganda of, 94–95; Schmitt on, 6–7

neoliberalism as anti-liberalism, 16–42; arbitrary power fostered by neoliberalism, 16–24; classical liberalism as restraint on neoliberalism and arbitrary power, 9–10, 24–31; neoliberalism, defined, 4, 18; uncensorable speech and anti-liberalism and illiberalism distinctions from, 44–46. *See also* corporate power

new conspiracism, 102–31; defined, 106–8; digital media corporations as gatekeepers and, 120–24; effect on political party rivalry and knowledge-producing institutions, 102–3; epistemic polarization from, 103, 109–11; free speech and, 103, 116, 120, 123–26; individual harm and civil remedies for, 114–20; of Pizzagate, 103–6, 110; speaking truth to conspiracy for, 111–14

New Deal, 71–72

New Yorker, "When Tyranny Takes Hold" (Osnos), 92

New York Times v. Sullivan (1964), 116

New York University, 83

Niemöller, Martin, 105

Nietzsche, F., 47

Nigeria, physical coercion by economic agents in, 22

9/11 attacks, 106

1960s radicalism, 46–50

Nobody Died at Sandy Hook (book), 118

nomenclature of neoliberalism, 38–39n4

Nyhan, Brendan, 112

Obama, Barack, 64, 109

Office of Information and Regulatory Affairs (Office of Management and Budget), 68

Office of Management and Budget (OMB), 68

oligarchy, 74n2

On Tyranny (Snyder), 82

Orban, Viktor, 3, 7, 8

Orte, Viscount of, 29

Orwell, George, 84

Osnos, Evan, 92, 123

otherness: authoritarianism and sovereign decisionism, 6–7; friend-enemy distinction, 7; George W. Bush on "enemy combatants," 6; "lost" migrant children and Trump administration, 128n30; race and principle of likeness, 5; "Soros/migrant" conspiracy, 105, 107, 111; Trump's "Muslim travel ban," 8. *See also* gender; Nazis and Third Reich; race

The Paranoid Style in America Politics (Hofstadter), 108

performative re-signification, 51–52

Phelan, Sean, 39n4

Pinochet, Augusto, 34–35

Plato, 1

Podesta, John, 103

Poland, rise of illiberalism in, 3, 7

political power. *See* post-truth and authoritarianism; state power

populism vs. technocracy, in administrative government, 62, 72–73, 74n2

pornography, Supreme Court's protection of, 4

Posner, Eric, 71

Post-Truth (McIntyre), 83

post-truth and authoritarianism, 78–101; authoritarianism and sovereign decisionism, 6–7; fake news, 79, 97–98n4, 98n19, 99n20; freedom of the press and, 82–86; January 6 insurrection, 95–97; motive for lying by authoritarians, 80–82; post-truth, defined, 78–79; propaganda as power, 79, 80, 89, 90; recent examples of, 89–92; repetition effect, 87, 94–95; rule of law and, 82, 86–89; uncensorable speech and illiberalism, 43, 58–60. *See also* new conspiracism

Powell, Lewis, 116
Pozner, Leonard, 102, 111–12, 115–16, 121
Pozner, Noah, 111, 115, 118
"presidentialism," 11, 66, 70–72, 76n21
propaganda: as power, 79, 80, 89, 90; repetition effect of, 87, 94–95. *See also* post-truth and authoritarianism
Putin, Vladimir, 80

QAnon, 96, 105, 110–11, 126n5

race: censorship enforced by legal system and, 50–52, 61n17; racist speech defended as free speech, 4–5
radical left, irony of, 46–50
Rawls, John, 1, 2, 19
regulation: neoliberalism and deregulation, 18 (*see also* neoliberalism as anti-liberalism); procedural protection of regulated private parties, 66–70; self-regulation vs. review of administration agencies, 76n20. *See also* administrative government and illiberalism
religion and political power, 28–29
repetition effect, 87, 94–95
Republican Party: conservatism as obedience to leaders, 91; conservatives on administrative government, 66–67, 70; new conspiracism and, 107–8, 113, 119; right-leaning weaponization of free speech, 7–9, 43–44, 57–58; 2020 presidential election and, 95, 96, 100n45. *See also* Trump, Donald
Reuters/Ipsos poll (2021), 108
Ricardo, David, 19
Rich, Joel and Mary, 118–19
Rich, Seth, 118–19
Richards, Lucy, 115
ricochet effect, 85–86
"The Rise of Illiberal Democracy" (Zakaria), 3

Rorty, Richard, 47–48, 59
Rosen, Jim, 83
Rosenblum, Nancy L., 102
Rosenbloom v. Metromedia Inc. (1971), 116
Rousseau, Jean-Jacques, 55
rule of law: fake news as threat to, 82, 86–89; legal grabs for power and, 90; violence of routine legal acts and, 52, 61n23
Russia, Special Counsel's Investigation (2016 election), 86–89
Rustow, Alexander, 20–21

salus populi (basic interests of the people), 25
Sandy Hook Elementary School, 102, 104, 110–12, 115–18, 121, 123
Saussure, Ferdinand de, 49–50, 60
Scarry, Elaine, 53–54
Schmidt, Steve, 91
Schmitt, Carl, 6–7, 52–53, 56, 58
Scott, Joan, 43
Second Amendment and new conspiracism, 116
self-regulation by administrative agencies, 76n20
separation of powers, 28, 41n56
Shell, 22
Slate, "Turkey's Warning" (Mounk), 100n43
Slobodian, Quinn, 39n13
Smith, Adam, 1, 19
Snyder, Timothy, 82
Soros, George, 105, 107, 111
sovereign decisionism, 6–7
Special Counsel's Investigation (2016 election), 86–89
The Spirit of the Laws (Montesquieu), 28–30
Stack, Kevin, 68
Stalin, Joseph, 80
Stanley, Jason, 43, 79
state power: as arbitrary, 41n61; religion and limitation of political power, 28–29; required for

Index

state power (*continued*)
  individual liberty, 1–3; separation of powers, 28, 41n56. *See also* post-truth and authoritarianism; *individual names of countries*
stealth revolution, 16
Sunstein, Cass, 93, 113
Supreme Court. *See* courts; *individual case names*
Szalay, Michael, 48

technocracy vs. populism, in administrative government, 62, 72–73, 74nn1–2
Texas, conspiracies about, 113, 129n54
Thatcher, Margaret, 35
They Thought They Were Free (Mayer), 90, 93
totalitarianism. *See* post-truth and authoritarianism
Toward a Feminist Theory of the State (MacKinnon), 4
trade unions and neoliberalism, 32–35
"tribal" belonging, 107–8
true-enoughness (verisimilitude), 24, 127
Trump, Donald: administrative government and illiberalism, 64, 72; neoliberalism and populism, 37; new conspiracism and, 103–5, 107–8, 110, 118, 121–23; post-truth and authoritarianism and, 79, 80, 83, 86–88, 91, 94–97, 101n57; rise of illiberalism and, 3, 7, 8–9; uncensorable speech and illiberalism, 43, 58–59. *See also* new conspiracism; post-truth and authoritarianism
Turkey: authoritarianism in, 89–91, 100n32; rise of illiberalism in, 3, 7; "Turkey's Warning" (Mounk), 100n43
Twitter, 9, 123

Ulukaya, Hamdi, 115
uncensorable speech. *See* free speech
United States Congress: congressional delegation to administrative government, 66–68, 70; executive branch polarized from, 64; impeachment power of, 87–88
United States Department of Justice, 8
United States executive branch: Congress polarized from, 64; free speech manipulated by, 8–9; "presidentialism," 11, 66, 70–72, 76n21. *See also individual names of presidents*
United States Supreme Court. *See* courts; *individual case names*
University of Iowa, 92
University of Pennsylvania, 98n9

Van Horn, Robert, 40n27
verisimilitude (true-enoughness), 24, 127
Vermeule, Adrian, 52, 65–66, 71, 113
violence: perpetrated by language, 49; of routine legal acts, 52, 61n23
voting. *See* elections and voting

Washington Post: Dionne on fake news, 81; "In a New Poll, Half of Republicans Say They Would Support Postponing the 2020 Election if Trump Proposed It," 100n45
Welch, Edgar, 104
"When Tyranny Takes Hold" (Osnos), 92
Whyte, Jessica, 34–35
"Will We Stop Trump Before It's Too Late" (Albright), 93–94
Wired, on *Gertz* decision, 117
Wizard of Oz effect, 35
"Women's Marches" (January 2017), 94

Yiannopolous, Milo, 123
YouTube, 104, 115, 122

Zakaria, Fareed, 3
Ziblatt, Daniel, 96–97
Zollinger, Bryan, 107
Zuckerberg, Mark, 121, 123–24